The **Galveston Diet**
Cookbook for Beginners

A Quick Path to Wellness: Easy & Fast Anti Inflammatory and Hormone Balancing Recipes

Martha McGrew

Disclaimer Notice:

The information provided in this book is for educational and informational purposes only and is not intended as a substitute for professional advice, therapy, or treatment. While every effort has been made to ensure the accuracy and effectiveness of the information in this book, the author and publisher make no guarantee as to the outcomes upon applying the ideas and techniques presented herein. The author and publisher shall have neither liability nor responsibility to any person or entity concerning any loss, damage, or injury caused or alleged to be caused directly or indirectly by the content of this book.

Thank You for Reading!

I hope you will enjoy reading it as much as I enjoyed writing it. <u>Your support means the world to me!</u>

If you will find value in these pages, I kindly ask you to consider **leaving an honest review on Amazon.** Your feedback not only helps me improve but also helps other readers discover this book.

YOUR GIFT IS WAITING FOR YOU!

TO ENHANCE YOUR GALVESTON DIET EXPERIENCE, WE'VE CRAFTED AN EXCEPTIONAL JOURNAL TAILORED TO TRACK YOUR MEALS, EMOTIONS, AND BODY CHANGES WITH EASE AND INSIGHT.

FIND DOWNLOAD INSTRUCTIONS AT THE END OF THE BOOK

WE'RE CONFIDENT YOU'LL LOVE THESE ADDITIONAL RESOURCES!

BONUS

Welcome to the Galveston Diet

Hello, and a warm welcome to your first step into a transformative journey - the Galveston Diet! I'm thrilled to walk this path with you, where we unveil a world where weight loss and wellness are not just dreams but achievable realities.

Have you ever stumbled upon a diet plan and wondered, "Is this the one that will finally work?" You're not alone. We've all been there - the starting lines of something promising, only to find it unsustainable or too complex. But here's where the Galveston Diet stands apart. It's not just a diet; it's a lifestyle change rooted in science, simplicity, and sustainability.

I remember Sarah, a dedicated professional juggling her career and family, her health taking a backseat. The story may sound familiar. Sarah was where you might be right now, searching for something effective yet easy to follow. And that's when the Galveston Diet graced her life.

In just a few months, Sarah waved goodbye to those persistent pounds and the constant feeling of fatigue. But it wasn't just about the numbers on the scale. She found her energy soaring, her skin glowing, and an overall sense of well-being that no fad diet ever gifted her. Sounds incredible, right?

The Galveston Diet is unique – it's not about starving or depriving yourself. It's about understanding your body, nourishing it with the right ingredients, and witnessing a transformation that goes beyond the physical. It's about anti-inflammatory foods that not only aid in shedding weight but also uplift your overall health.

I know the skepticism that creeps in – I've been there. But the beauty of the Galveston Diet is its foundation in science. It's not a whimsical approach but a meticulously crafted path, each element backed by research, each recipe designed to be your ally in this journey to wellness.

So, are you ready to embrace a version of yourself that feels invincible, energetic, and vibrant? This isn't just another diet book. It's your companion, your guide, a testament to the fact that the ideal version of ourselves is attainable and sustainable.

I can't wait to embark on this exciting journey with you. A world of wellness, energy, and vitality awaits – let's step in, together.

TABLE OF CONTENTS

What is the Galveston Diet?

The Galveston Diet was developed by Dr. Mary Claire Haver, an experienced obstetrician-gynecologist, in the coastal Texas city of Galveston. She created it to help women manage common symptoms during menopause like weight gain, hot flashes, night sweats, mood changes, and fatigue. Unlike trendy diets that promise fast results through extreme restrictions, the Galveston Diet takes a more holistic, maintainable approach to women's health and well-being during this transition. It focuses on making gradual shifts to better nutrition, adequate physical activity, stress relief practices, and lifestyle habits that support women through menopause and beyond. The Galveston Diet aims to help women adapt their lifestyles for long-term balance and quality of life.

The Core Principles

1. Anti-Inflammatory Foods:
A core principle of the Galveston Diet is emphasizing anti-inflammatory foods. While some inflammation is a normal bodily process, excessive levels can worsen menopausal symptoms and contribute to various health problems. The diet encourages plentiful intake of antioxidant-rich foods like berries, leafy greens, nuts, and fatty fish to help combat inflammation. These foods, abundant in compounds that neutralize cell-damaging free radicals, are the foundation of the Galveston Diet's nutritional guidance. By spotlighting anti-inflammatory foods, the diet aims to relieve menopausal symptoms and promote overall wellness during this transition.

2. Intermittent Fasting:
In addition to anti-inflammatory foods, intermittent fasting is a key part of the Galveston Diet. This involves alternating intervals of fasting and eating within a defined timeframe. Intermittent fasting is thought to enhance weight loss, boost metabolic health, and provide other wellness perks.

So, the Galveston Diet doesn't just focus on nutritional choices - it also guides meal timing and fasting periods. By incorporating intermittent fasting, the diet introduces an element of discipline around when, not just what, to eat. This fasting component is believed to complement the diet's anti-inflammatory food recommendations.

3. Macronutrient Balance:
Recognizing that each woman's body is unique, the Galveston Diet can be customized as needed. While it recommends balancing protein, fat, and carbohydrate intake, flexibility is important. The diet advises women to tune into their bodies and tweak their macro ratios based on their particular needs, objectives, and reactions to certain foods. Rather than a rigid, one-size-fits-all plan, the Galveston Diet enables women to take a personalized approach and adjust their dietary choices according to what works best for their bodies during menopause. By allowing for individualization, the diet acknowledges the differences between women's bodies at this life stage.

Beyond Weight Loss
Although weight loss is a frequent objective, the Galveston Diet takes a broader view of wellness. It has a strong educational element, aiming to give women knowledge about the physical changes and shifting nutritional requirements during menopause. While the diet can aid weight management, it also targets increased energy, better mood, enhanced sleep quality, and overall well-being. These are important goals for women experiencing the ups and downs of menopause. Rather than focusing narrowly on pounds shed, the Galveston Diet seeks to provide women with information, tools, and support to thrive holistically through the menopausal transition and beyond. The educational foundation empowers women to take charge of their health.

Benefits of the Galveston Diet

As you embark on this journey of transformation and discovery, it is crucial to understand the myriad of benefits that await you. The Galveston Diet, designed meticulously with menopausal women in mind, promises more than weight management; it is a comprehensive lifestyle change advocating holistic wellness.

Nutritional Revitalization

1. Anti-Inflammatory Rich Menu

One of the quintessential benefits of the Galveston Diet is the focus on anti-inflammatory foods. Each recipe in this cookbook is crafted to not only tantalize your taste buds but also to flood your body with nutrients that combat inflammation. You'll find a plethora of dishes rich in antioxidants, ensuring that every meal contributes to reducing inflammation, promoting overall well-being, and making each day a step towards vibrancy and health.

2. Balanced Macronutrients

The Galveston Diet emphasizes a harmonious balance of proteins, fats, and carbohydrates. This balance is not just pivotal for weight loss but also for enhancing energy levels and cognitive function. Each recipe adheres to this principle, offering a balanced plate that fuels your body and mind, meeting the unique needs of women transitioning through menopause.

Physiological Rejuvenation

3. Weight Management

As you delve into the curated selection of recipes, you'll discover the ease with which weight management can be integrated into your lifestyle. The combination of anti-inflammatory foods and intermittent fasting propels weight loss, addresses stubborn midlife weight gain, and ushers a phase of revitalization.

4. Hormonal Balance

Menopause heralds a time of significant hormonal changes. The Galveston Diet, through its intricate blend of nutrients, works to mitigate the impacts of these fluctuations. Women who embrace this diet report reduced severity of hot flashes, improved mood stability, and enhanced overall hormonal equilibrium.

Psychological and Emotional Well-being

5. Mood Enhancement

The connection between diet and mood is undeniable. The Galveston Diet's rich nutrient profile promotes enhanced mental health. Each bite is a step towards not just physical, but also emotional and psychological well-being, ensuring that the menopausal journey is navigated with grace, strength, and vitality.

Tips for Following the Galveston Diet

To fully benefit from the Galveston Diet and make it a smooth part of your life, here are some key tips to empower your journey:

1. Educate Yourself

Learn all you can about the diet's principles so you can make informed choices aligned with your goals and your health needs.

2. Customize Your Journey

Customize the diet to fit your unique body, needs, and preferences. Be flexible and listen to what your body responds best to.

3. Embrace Intermittent Fasting

Ease into intermittent fasting if new to it. Start with shorter periods, building up as your body adjusts. Be patient and kind to yourself.

4. Anti-Inflammatory Foods Are Your Allies

Explore anti-inflammatory foods for a nutritious and tasty diet variety. Use recipes in this book as inspiration for your creations.

5. Stay Hydrated

Stay hydrated, especially during fasting. Water aids metabolism, radiant skin, and bodily functions.

6. Join the Community

Connect with others on this journey for support, advice, and community empowerment.

7. Regular Exercise

Couple the diet with regular exercise you enjoy to complement the nutrition.

8. Consult a Professional

Consider consulting a professional to personalize the diet to your health status.

9. Journal Your Journey

Keep a journal to track your meals, and note your emotional and physical changes.

10. Patience and Compassion

Have patience and self-compassion. This is a journey, not a destination. Celebrate small victories, as each step forward is a triumph.

Breakfast and Smoothies

Welcome, dear reader, to a pivotal section of "The Galveston Diet for Beginners," where we embark on a delightful journey through the vibrant world of breakfast and smoothies. I'm thrilled to be your guide, as we explore nourishing recipes that not only tantalize the taste buds but also align perfectly with the core principles of the Galveston diet. Every sip, every bite, is a step towards a healthier, more radiant you.

In the quiet calm of the morning, when the world is just awakening from its slumber, there's an intimate magic to the first meal of the day. It's not just about silencing the rumblings of a fasting stomach; it's a serene moment where we nurture our body and spirit, setting the tone for the hours to come. And isn't it wonderful that with the Galveston diet, every breakfast is a harmonious blend of nutrition, flavor, and joy?

Bursting with Nutrients
Our curated selection of recipes is a colorful palette of fresh, wholesome ingredients that come together in a symphony of flavors. Each recipe is crafted with precision, ensuring it's not only delectable but also rich in nutrients that align with the Galveston diet's essence. We've weaved in the art and science of this renowned diet to ensure each meal energizes your body and awakens your senses.

Smoothie Magic
Imagine starting your day with a glass brimming with the vibrant hues of nature's bounty. Our smoothies are not just drinks; they're experiences. Each sip is a dance of flavors, where fruits, vegetables, and special ingredients intermingle, bringing you not just refreshment but nourishment that lasts. Whether you're in the mood for something tropical and zesty or creamy and indulgent - we've got you covered.

Building Blocks of Well-being
As we journey through this section together, remember, that each recipe is more than a list of ingredients and steps. It's a building block of your well-being, a testament to the transformative power of the Galveston diet. We've ensured diversity and simplicity, offering you an array of choices that cater to every palate, schedule, and dietary preference.

Join Us!
So, let's turn the page, shall we? A world of aromatic, flavorful, and nourishing breakfasts and smoothies awaits. Together, we'll explore, taste, and savor – each recipe a step closer to wellness, vitality, and the radiant health that the Galveston diet promises. With every sunrise, let's usher in a day of energy, clarity, and vibrancy. Are you ready to step into a world where every breakfast is a celebration of taste and health? Your journey to delightful mornings and energized days begins now!

Morning Sunshine Smoothie Bowl

Preparation Time: 10 minutes | Cooking Time: 0 minutes | Portion Size: 1 serving

Ingredients:

- 1 ripe banana
- ½ cup frozen mango chunks
- ½ cup frozen pineapple chunks
- 1 tablespoon chia seeds
- ½ cup unsweetened almond milk
- Toppings: sliced almonds, coconut flakes, fresh berries

Instructions:

1. In a high-powered blender, combine the banana, frozen mango, frozen pineapple, chia seeds, and almond milk.
2. Blend on high until smooth and creamy. If the mixture is too thick, you can add a little more almond milk to reach your desired consistency.
3. Pour the smoothie into a bowl.
4. Garnish with a sprinkle of sliced almonds, coconut flakes, and fresh berries to your liking.
5. Serve immediately and enjoy the burst of flavors and energy to kickstart your day!

Nutritional Data:

Calories: 320 | Protein: 8g | Carbs: 55g | Fat: 9g | Fiber: 12g | Sugar: 30g

Avocado & Egg Protein Boost Toast

Preparation Time: 5 minutes | Cooking Time: 5 minutes | Portion Size: 1 serving

Ingredients:

- 1 slice of whole-grain bread
- ½ ripe avocado
- 1 large egg
- 1 teaspoon olive oil
- Salt and pepper to taste
- Optional toppings: red pepper flakes, chopped herbs

Instructions:

1. Toast the slice of whole-grain bread to your preference.
2. While the bread is toasting, heat the olive oil in a non-stick skillet over medium heat.
3. Crack the egg into the skillet and cook to your liking (sunny side up, over-easy, or scrambled).
4. Mash the ripe avocado and spread it evenly over the toasted bread.
5. Place the cooked egg on top of the avocado layer.
6. Season with salt and pepper to taste. For extra flavor, sprinkle red pepper flakes or freshly chopped herbs if desired.
7. Serve immediately and enjoy a protein-packed, flavorful breakfast!

Nutritional Data:

Calories: 370 | Protein: 12g | Carbs: 23g | Fat: 27g | Fiber: 9g | Sugar: 3g

Blueberry Bliss Almond Oatmeal

Preparation Time: 5 minutes | Cooking Time: 10 minutes | Portion Size: 1 serving

Ingredients:

- ½ cup rolled oats
- 1 cup unsweetened almond milk
- ½ cup fresh blueberries
- 1 tablespoon almond butter
- 1 tablespoon honey or maple syrup (optional)

- A sprinkle of chia seeds (optional)

Instructions:

1. In a small saucepan, bring the almond milk to a low boil.
2. Add the rolled oats, reduce the heat, and simmer, stirring occasionally until the oats are soft and have absorbed most of the milk, about 5-7 minutes.
3. While the oats are cooking, you can optionally toast the almond butter in a small pan over medium heat until it becomes warm and slightly runny.
4. Remove the oatmeal from the heat and let it sit for a minute to thicken.
5. Pour the oatmeal into a bowl, and drizzle with the warm almond butter and honey or maple syrup if desired.
6. Top with fresh blueberries and a sprinkle of chia seeds for an extra nutrient boost.
7. Serve immediately and enjoy the warm, comforting, and nutritious breakfast!

Nutritional Data:

Calories: 350 | Protein: 9g | Carbs: 45g | Fat: 15g | Fiber: 8g | Sugar: 17g (if honey is added)

Tropical Coconut Chia Pudding

Preparation Time: 10 minutes | Cooking Time: 0 minutes (but needs to chill for at least 2 hours) | Portion Size: 1 serving

Ingredients:

- 3 tablespoons chia seeds
- 1 cup coconut milk
- ½ teaspoon vanilla extract
- 1 tablespoon honey or maple syrup (optional)
- ½ cup diced mango
- ½ cup diced pineapple
- 2 tablespoons shredded coconut

Instructions:

1. In a bowl, mix chia seeds with coconut milk, vanilla extract, and honey or maple syrup if desired. Stir well to combine.
2. Cover the bowl and place it in the refrigerator for at least 2 hours or overnight to let the chia seeds absorb the liquid and gel, forming a pudding-like consistency.
3. Once the chia pudding is set, give it a good stir to break up any clumps.
4. In a serving bowl, layer the chia pudding with diced mango and pineapple.
5. Top with a sprinkle of shredded coconut for a touch of tropical flavor.
6. Serve immediately and enjoy this refreshing and nutritious treat!

Nutritional Data:

Calories: 400 | Protein: 8g | Carbs: 40g | Fat: 25g | Fiber: 12g | Sugar: 25g (if honey is added)

Savory Spinach and Mushroom Frittata

Preparation Time: 10 minutes | Cooking Time: 20 minutes | Portion Size: 2 servings

Ingredients:

- 4 large eggs
- 1 cup fresh spinach, chopped
- 1 cup mushrooms, sliced
- 1 small onion, diced
- 2 tablespoons olive oil
- Salt and pepper to taste
- 2 tablespoons grated Parmesan cheese (optional)

Instructions:

1. Preheat the oven to 350°F (175°C).
2. In a medium oven-safe skillet, heat the olive oil over medium heat.
3. Add the diced onions and sliced mushrooms, sautéing until they are softened, about 5-7 minutes.

4. In the meantime, in a bowl, whisk together the eggs, salt, and pepper.

5. Pour the egg mixture over the sautéed onions and mushrooms in the skillet.

6. Sprinkle the chopped spinach evenly over the top.

7. Allow the eggs to set a bit on the edges, then sprinkle with grated Parmesan cheese if desired.

8. Transfer the skillet to the preheated oven and bake for about 10-12 minutes, or until the eggs are set and the top is lightly golden.

9. Remove from the oven, let it cool for a couple of minutes, then slice and serve. Enjoy your delicious and nutritious breakfast!

Nutritional Data:

Calories: 290 | Protein: 15g | Carbs: 8g | Fat: 23g | Fiber: 2g | Sugar: 4g

Golden Turmeric Breakfast Muffin

Preparation Time: 15 minutes | Cooking Time: 20 minutes | Portion Size: 12 muffins

Ingredients:

- 2 cups almond flour
- 1 teaspoon baking powder
- 3 large eggs
- 1/4 cup coconut oil, melted
- 1/4 cup honey or maple syrup
- 1 teaspoon vanilla extract
- 2 teaspoons turmeric powder
- 1 teaspoon cinnamon
- 1/2 teaspoon ground ginger
- 1/4 teaspoon black pepper
- 1/2 cup raisins or chopped nuts (optional)

Instructions:

1. Preheat your oven to 350°F (175°C) and line a muffin tin with paper liners or grease with a bit of coconut oil.

2. In a large mixing bowl, whisk together the almond flour, baking powder, turmeric, cinnamon, ground ginger, and black pepper.

3. In another bowl, mix the eggs, melted coconut oil, honey or maple syrup, and vanilla extract until well combined.

4. Pour the wet ingredients into the dry ingredients and stir until just combined. Be careful not to overmix; it's okay if a few lumps are remaining.

5. If desired, fold in the raisins or chopped nuts to add a bit of texture and extra flavor to your muffins.

6. Spoon the batter into the prepared muffin tin, filling each cup about 2/3 of the way full.

7. Bake for 18-20 minutes, or until the tops are golden and a toothpick inserted into the center of a muffin comes out clean.

8. Allow the muffins to cool in the tin for about 5 minutes, then transfer them to a wire rack to cool completely.

9. Enjoy a golden turmeric muffin with a cup of tea

Nutritional Data:

Calories: 181 | Protein: 5g | Carbs: 9g | Fat: 14g | Fiber: 2g | Sugar: 5g

Nutty Banana Breakfast Bars

Preparation Time: 15 minutes | Cooking Time: 20 minutes | Portion Size: 12 bars

Ingredients:

- 2 ripe bananas, mashed
- 1 cup rolled oats
- ½ cup almond flour
- ¼ cup mixed nuts chopped (e.g., almonds, walnuts, pecans)
- ¼ cup unsweetened almond butter
- 2 tablespoons honey or maple syrup
- 1 teaspoon vanilla extract
- ½ teaspoon cinnamon
- ¼ teaspoon salt

Instructions:

1. Preheat the oven to 350°F (175°C), and line an 8-inch square baking pan with parchment paper, leaving an overhang on two opposite sides (this helps in lifting the bars out later).
2. In a large mixing bowl, combine the mashed bananas, rolled oats, almond flour, chopped nuts, almond butter, honey or maple syrup, vanilla extract, cinnamon, and salt. Stir well until all ingredients are thoroughly combined.
3. Transfer the mixture to the prepared baking pan and use a spatula to press it down evenly.
4. Bake for 20-25 minutes, or until the edges start to turn golden brown and a toothpick inserted into the center comes out clean.
5. Allow the bars to cool in the pan for about 10 minutes, then use the parchment paper overhangs to lift them out and transfer them to a wire rack to cool completely.
6. Once cooled, use a sharp knife to cut into 12 equal bars.
7. Enjoy these Nutty Banana Breakfast Bars as a quick breakfast option or a snack on the go!

Nutritional Data:

Calories: 150 | Protein: 4g | Carbs: 18g | Fat: 7g | Fiber: 3g | Sugar: 8g

Zesty Lemon Berry Parfait

Preparation Time: 10 minutes | Cooking Time: 0 minutes | Portion Size: 2 servings

Ingredients:

- 1 cup Greek yogurt, unsweetened
- 1 tablespoon honey or maple syrup (optional)
- 1 teaspoon lemon zest
- 2 tablespoons lemon juice
- 1 cup mixed berries (e.g., strawberries, blueberries, raspberries)
- 2 tablespoons granola, no added sugar

- 1 tablespoon chia seeds

Instructions:

1. In a bowl, mix the Greek yogurt with honey or maple syrup (if using), lemon zest, and lemon juice. Stir well until the mixture is smooth and creamy.
2. In serving glasses or bowls, start layering the parfait. Begin with a layer of the lemony yogurt mixture.
3. Add a layer of mixed berries on top of the yogurt.
4. Sprinkle a layer of granola over the berries, then add a small dollop of yogurt on top.
5. Repeat the layers until the glasses are filled, usually about two layers depending on the size of your serving glasses.
6. Finish off with a layer of berries, and sprinkle chia seeds on top for an added nutritional boost.
7. Serve immediately and enjoy this refreshing, zesty, and nutritious breakfast!

Nutritional Data:

Calories: 180 | Protein: 11g | Carbs: 25g (without added sweetener) | Fat: 5g | Fiber: 5g | Sugar: 15g (without added sweetener)

Green Goddess Veggie Omelette

Preparation Time: 10 minutes | Cooking Time: 8 minutes | Portion Size: 1 serving

Ingredients:

- 2 large eggs
- 1 tablespoon olive oil
- 1/4 cup spinach, chopped
- 1/4 cup broccoli florets, chopped
- 1/4 cup green bell pepper, diced
- 1/4 cup zucchini, diced
- 2 tablespoons feta cheese, crumbled (optional)
- Salt and pepper to taste
- Fresh herbs (like parsley or chives) for garnish, chopped

Instructions:

1. In a bowl, beat the eggs and season with a pinch of salt and pepper. Set aside.
2. Heat the olive oil in a non-stick skillet over medium heat.
3. Add the broccoli, green bell pepper, and zucchini to the skillet. Sauté the vegetables for about 3-4 minutes, or until they are slightly tender.
4. Add the spinach and cook for an additional minute, until the spinach is wilted.
5. Spread the vegetables evenly across the skillet. Pour the beaten eggs over the vegetables, ensuring the veggies are covered evenly.
6. Allow the eggs to cook undisturbed for 2-3 minutes until they start to set around the edges.
7. Sprinkle the crumbled feta cheese over the top of the omelette, if using.
8. Use a spatula to lift the edges of the omelette gently and check if it's easy to flip. If ready, flip the omelette and cook for an additional 2-3 minutes until the eggs are fully cooked.
9. Slide the omelette onto a plate, and garnish with fresh chopped herbs.
10. Serve immediately and enjoy your nutrient-packed, colorful, and flavorful breakfast!

Nutritional Data:

Calories: 300 | Protein: 18g | Carbs: 10g | Fat: 22g | Fiber: 3g | Sugar: 5g

Cinnamon Apple Almond Porridge

Preparation Time: 5 minutes | Cooking Time: 10 minutes | Portion Size: 2 servings

Ingredients:

- 1 cup almond flour
- 2 cups unsweetened almond milk
- 1 apple, peeled, cored, and diced
- 1 tablespoon almond butter
- 2 teaspoons cinnamon
- 1 tablespoon chia seeds
- Optional: a drizzle of honey or maple syrup, and a sprinkle of sliced almonds for garnish

Instructions:

1. In a saucepan, combine the almond milk and almond flour over medium heat. Whisk continuously to ensure a smooth texture, heating for about 5 minutes until it starts to thicken.
2. While the almond mixture is heating, place another small pan over medium heat and add the diced apples and cinnamon. Cook the apples for about 5 minutes until they become tender, stirring occasionally.
3. Once the almond mixture has thickened to a porridge-like consistency, remove it from the heat and stir in the almond butter and chia seeds until well combined.
4. Divide the porridge into two bowls. Top with the cinnamon-cooked apples. If desired, add a drizzle of honey or maple syrup and a sprinkle of sliced almonds for extra texture and flavor.
5. Serve immediately and enjoy the warm, comforting, and nourishing breakfast!

Nutritional Data:

Calories: 350 | Protein: 12g | Carbs: 25g | Fat: 24g | Fiber: 10g | Sugar: 12g (excluding optional sweeteners)

Kale & Kiwi Superfood Smoothie

Preparation Time: 5 minutes | Cooking Time: 0 minutes | Portion Size: 1 serving

Ingredients:

- 1 cup kale leaves, stems removed
- 1 ripe kiwi, peeled and sliced
- 1/2 banana
- 1 tablespoon chia seeds
- 1 tablespoon flax seeds
- 1 cup unsweetened almond milk
- 1 teaspoon honey or maple syrup (optional)
- Ice cubes (optional)

Instructions:

1. In a blender, add the kale leaves and unsweetened almond milk. Blend until the kale is fully broken down into small pieces.
2. Add the sliced kiwi and banana to the blender. Blend again until the fruits are fully incorporated, and the mixture becomes smooth.
3. Incorporate chia seeds and flax seeds into the blend, adding a boost of fiber and omega-3 fatty acids.
4. If desired, add a teaspoon of honey or maple syrup to sweeten and ice cubes to make it more refreshing. Blend until everything is smooth and well combined.
5. Pour the smoothie into a glass, and it's ready to enjoy immediately! For an extra touch, garnish with a slice of kiwi or a sprinkle of chia seeds on top.

Nutritional Data:

Calories: 220 | Protein: 8g | Carbs: 35g | Fat: 8g | Fiber: 10g | Sugar: 15g (excluding optional sweeteners)

Sweet Potato and Spinach Breakfast Hash

Preparation Time: 10 minutes | Cooking Time: 20 minutes | Portion Size: 2 servings

Ingredients:

- 1 medium sweet potato, peeled and diced
- 2 cups fresh spinach, roughly chopped
- 1 small onion, diced
- 2 cloves garlic, minced
- 2 tablespoons olive oil
- 2 large eggs (optional)
- Salt and pepper to taste
- 1 teaspoon smoked paprika
- Fresh herbs for garnish (e.g., parsley, chives)

Instructions:

1. Heat the olive oil in a large skillet over medium heat. Add the diced sweet potatoes and cook for about 10-12 minutes, stirring occasionally until they are slightly tender and golden brown.
2. Add the diced onion and minced garlic to the skillet. Cook for another 3-4 minutes until the onions become soft and translucent.
3. Sprinkle the smoked paprika, salt, and pepper over the sweet potatoes and onions, mixing well to evenly distribute the spices.
4. Add the chopped spinach to the skillet, stirring until the spinach is wilted and incorporated into the hash.
5. If desired, make two wells in the hash and crack an egg into each. Cover the skillet and let it cook for another 3-4 minutes until the eggs are cooked to your liking.
6. Remove the skillet from the heat, and use a spatula to divide the hash between two plates.
7. Garnish with fresh herbs for an added touch of flavor and serve immediately. Enjoy this warm, hearty, and nutritious breakfast!

Nutritional Data:

Calories: 300 | Protein: 8g (without eggs) 16g (with eggs) | Carbs: 35g | Fat: 15g | Fiber: 6g | Sugar: 9g

Creamy Almond Butter & Berry Toast

Preparation Time: 5 minutes | Cooking Time: 2 minutes | Portion Size: 1 serving

Ingredients:

- 1 slice of whole-grain bread or gluten-free bread, as per preference
- 2 tablespoons almond butter
- 1/4 cup mixed berries (like strawberries, blueberries, and raspberries)
- 1 teaspoon chia seeds
- 1 teaspoon honey or maple syrup (optional)
- A sprinkle of cinnamon (optional)

Instructions:

1. Toast the slice of bread to your liking.
2. While the bread is toasting, wash and prepare the mixed berries. If using strawberries, slice them thinly.
3. Spread the almond butter evenly over the toasted bread.
4. Arrange the mixed berries on top of the almond butter layer, creating a colorful and appetizing array.
5. If desired, drizzle a teaspoon of honey or maple syrup over the berries for a touch of natural sweetness.
6. Sprinkle chia seeds over the top, adding a bit of crunch and a nutritional boost.
7. For an extra touch of flavor, sprinkle a little cinnamon over the toast.
8. Serve immediately and savor every bite of this delicious, nutritious, and satisfying breakfast or snack!

Nutritional Data:

Calories: 280 | Protein: 9g | Carbs: 30g (without optional sweeteners) | Fat: 15g | Fiber: 8g | Sugar: 10g (without optional sweeteners)

Sunrise Quinoa and Fruit Salad

Preparation Time: 10 minutes | Cooking Time: 15 minutes | Portion Size: 4 servings

Ingredients:

- 1 cup quinoa, rinsed and drained
- 2 cups water
- 1 cup strawberries, hulled and sliced
- 1 orange, peeled and segmented
- 1/2 cup blueberries
- 1/2 cup pomegranate arils
- 2 tablespoons almond slices
- 2 tablespoons honey or maple syrup (optional)
- 1 teaspoon lemon zest
- Fresh mint leaves for garnish

Instructions:

1. In a medium saucepan, bring 2 cups of water to a boil. Add the rinsed quinoa, reduce the heat to low, cover, and cook for 12-15 minutes or until the quinoa is cooked through and the water is absorbed. Remove from heat and let it sit, covered, for an additional 5 minutes.
2. Fluff the cooked quinoa with a fork and let it cool to room temperature. You can expedite this process by spreading it out on a baking sheet.
3. In a large mixing bowl, combine the cooled quinoa, sliced strawberries, orange segments, blueberries, and pomegranate arils.
4. Drizzle the honey or maple syrup (if using) over the fruit and quinoa mixture and gently toss to combine everything well.
5. Garnish with almond slices, lemon zest, and fresh mint leaves for a refreshing touch.
6. Serve immediately or refrigerate for later use. This fruit and quinoa salad can be enjoyed as a refreshing breakfast, snack, or even a dessert!

Nutritional Data:

Calories: 220 | Protein: 6g | Carbs: 42g (without optional sweeteners) | Fat: 4g | Fiber: 6g | Sugar: 14g (without optional sweeteners)

Minty Melon and Walnut Yogurt Bowl

Preparation Time: 10 minutes | Cooking Time: 0 minutes | Portion Size: 2 servings

Ingredients:

- 1 cup Greek yogurt, unsweetened
- 1 cup mixed melon balls (cantaloupe, honeydew, watermelon)
- 1/4 cup walnuts, chopped
- 1 tablespoon honey or maple syrup (optional)
- 2 tablespoons fresh mint leaves, chopped
- 1 tablespoon chia seeds

Instructions:

1. Divide the Greek yogurt between two bowls, smoothing it into an even layer at the base of each bowl.
2. Arrange the mixed melon balls attractively on top of the yogurt in both bowls.
3. Sprinkle the chopped walnuts evenly over the melon and yogurt.
4. If desired, drizzle a tablespoon of honey or maple syrup over the top for a touch of sweetness.
5. Sprinkle the freshly chopped mint leaves over each bowl, adding a refreshing, aromatic touch to the dish.
6. Add a sprinkle of chia seeds over the top for an extra dose of fiber and omega-3 fatty acids.
7. Serve immediately and enjoy the delightful combination of creamy yogurt, crunchy walnuts, juicy melon, and refreshing mint. A beautiful start to your day!

Nutritional Data:

Calories: 290 | Protein: 15g | Carbs: 25g (without optional sweeteners) | Fat: 15g | Fiber: 5g | Sugar: 18g (without optional sweeteners)

Ginger Spice Overnight Oats

Preparation Time: 10 minutes | Cooking Time: 0 minutes (refrigeration overnight) | Portion Size: 2 servings

Ingredients:

- 1 cup rolled oats, gluten-free if necessary
- 1 cup almond milk, unsweetened
- 1 tablespoon chia seeds
- 2 tablespoons almond butter
- 1 teaspoon ground ginger
- 1/2 teaspoon cinnamon
- 1 tablespoon honey or maple syrup (optional)
- 1 apple, grated
- 2 tablespoons sliced almonds for garnish

Instructions:

1. In a mixing bowl, combine the rolled oats, chia seeds, ground ginger, and cinnamon. Mix well to distribute the spices evenly through the oats.
2. Add the almond milk and almond butter to the oats mixture. Mix well to combine, ensuring the almond butter is well integrated into the liquid and oat mixture.
3. Grate the apple and add it to the mixture, stirring to combine. The natural juices of the apple will also add moisture and sweetness to the oats.
4. If desired, sweeten the oats mixture with a tablespoon of honey or maple syrup, and mix well.
5. Divide the mixture into two serving jars or bowls. Cover them and place them in the refrigerator overnight, allowing the oats to absorb the liquid and the flavors to meld together.
6. In the morning, remove the oats from the refrigerator. They should be soft, creamy, and ready to eat.
7. Garnish the tops of the overnight oats with sliced almonds, adding a pleasant crunch and nutty flavor.

8. Enjoy your Ginger Spice Overnight Oats cold, straight from the fridge, for a refreshing and satisfying breakfast!

Nutritional Data:

Calories: 370 | **Protein:** 12g | **Carbs:** 50g (without optional sweeteners) | **Fat:** 15g | **Fiber:** 11g | Sugar: 15g (without optional sweeteners)

Fluffy Almond Pancakes with Mixed Berries

Preparation Time: 10 minutes | Cooking Time: 15 minutes | Portion Size: 2 servings (6 pancakes)

Ingredients:

- 1 cup almond flour
- 2 large eggs
- 1/4 cup unsweetened almond milk
- 1 teaspoon vanilla extract
- 1/2 teaspoon baking powder
- 1 tablespoon coconut oil, for cooking
- 1 cup mixed berries (strawberries, blueberries, raspberries)
- 1 tablespoon almond slivers, for garnish
- 1 teaspoon honey or maple syrup, optional

Instructions:

1. In a mixing bowl, whisk together the almond flour and baking powder. Ensure it's well combined to avoid clumps.
2. In another bowl, beat the eggs, then add the almond milk and vanilla extract, mixing well.
3. Pour the wet ingredients into the dry ingredients and stir until just combined. Be careful not to overmix; it's okay if there are a few lumps.
4. Heat a non-stick skillet or griddle over medium heat and add a bit of coconut oil to grease the surface.
5. Pour about a quarter cup of batter onto the skillet for each pancake. Cook for 2-3 minutes on one side until bubbles appear on the surface, then flip and cook for another 2 minutes on the other side.
6. While the pancakes are cooking, wash and prepare the mixed berries.
7. Serve the pancakes warm, topped with the fresh mixed berries. Sprinkle almond slivers on top for an extra crunch.
8. If desired, drizzle a teaspoon of honey or maple syrup over the top for added sweetness.
9. Enjoy the soft, fluffy almond pancakes with the juicy burst of fresh berries as a delightful Galveston diet-approved breakfast!

Nutritional Data:

Calories: 390 | **Protein:** 15g | **Carbs:** 20g (without optional sweeteners) | **Fat:** 30g | **Fiber:** 8g | Sugar: 10g (without optional sweeteners)

Cherry Almond Breakfast Cookies

Preparation Time: 15 minutes | Cooking Time: 12 minutes | Portion Size: 12 cookies

Ingredients:

- 1 cup almond flour
- 1/2 cup rolled oats, gluten-free if necessary
- 1/2 teaspoon baking powder
- 1/4 teaspoon salt

- 1/3 cup chopped dried cherries, unsweetened
- 1/4 cup almond slivers
- 2 large eggs
- 3 tablespoons coconut oil, melted
- 2 tablespoons honey or maple syrup
- 1 teaspoon vanilla extract

Instructions:

1. Preheat the oven to 350°F (175°C). Line a baking sheet with parchment paper.
2. In a large mixing bowl, combine almond flour, rolled oats, baking powder, and salt.
3. Stir in the chopped dried cherries and almond slivers into the dry mixture.
4. In another bowl, whisk together the eggs, melted coconut oil, honey or maple syrup, and vanilla extract until well combined.
5. Pour the wet ingredients into the dry ingredients and mix until just combined. Be careful not to overmix.
6. Use a cookie scoop or a tablespoon to drop dollops of the cookie dough onto the prepared baking sheet, spacing them about 2 inches apart.
7. Gently flatten each cookie dollop with the back of the spoon or your fingers.
8. Bake for 10-12 minutes, or until the edges of the cookies are lightly golden.
9. Allow the cookies to cool on the baking sheet for about 5 minutes, then transfer them to a wire rack to cool completely.
10. Enjoy these tasty, nutrient-packed breakfast cookies as a quick breakfast or a snack!

Nutritional Data:

Calories: 150 | Protein: 4g | Carbs: 12g | Fat: 10g | Fiber: 2g | Sugar: 7g

Refreshing Cucumber & Avocado Salad

Preparation Time: 10 minutes | Cooking Time: 0 minutes | Portion Size: 4 servings

Ingredients:

- 2 large cucumbers, sliced
- 2 ripe avocados, diced
- 1/4 cup red onion, thinly sliced
- 2 tablespoons extra-virgin olive oil
- 1 tablespoon apple cider vinegar
- Salt and pepper to taste
- 2 tablespoons fresh cilantro, chopped
- 1 tablespoon sesame seeds

Instructions:

1. In a large mixing bowl, combine the sliced cucumbers, diced avocados, and sliced red onions.
2. In a small bowl, whisk together the extra-virgin olive oil and apple cider vinegar. Add salt and pepper to taste, and mix well.
3. Drizzle the dressing over the cucumber, avocado, and onion mixture. Toss gently to coat the ingredients evenly with the dressing.
4. Sprinkle the fresh, chopped cilantro over the salad, lending a pop of color and a burst of fresh flavor.
5. Garnish with sesame seeds for a delightful crunch and added visual appeal.
6. Serve the salad immediately, or refrigerate for about 30 minutes to let the flavors meld together for an even more refreshing taste.
7. Enjoy this crisp, creamy, and refreshing salad as a light appetizer, side dish, or a quick, nutritious snack!

Nutritional Data:

Calories: 220 | Protein: 3g | Carbs: 12g | Fat: 19g | Fiber: 7g | Sugar: 3g

Warm Pecan and Apple Breakfast Bowl

Preparation Time: 10 minutes | Cooking Time: 5 minutes | Portion Size: 2 servings

Ingredients:

- 1 large apple, diced
- 1/2 cup pecans, chopped
- 1 tablespoon coconut oil
- 1 teaspoon cinnamon
- 1/2 teaspoon nutmeg
- 1 cup cooked quinoa
- 2 tablespoons almond butter
- 1 tablespoon chia seeds
- Optional: A drizzle of honey or maple syrup for added sweetness

Instructions:

1. In a medium skillet, melt the coconut oil over medium heat. Add the diced apples and cook for about 2-3 minutes until they begin to soften.
2. Stir in the chopped pecans, cinnamon, and nutmeg, and sauté for an additional 2 minutes until the apples are tender and the pecans are toasted.
3. While the apple and pecans are cooking, warm the cooked quinoa in a separate pan or microwave.
4. Divide the warm quinoa between two bowls, creating a comforting and wholesome base for the breakfast bowl.
5. Spoon the warm apple and pecan mixture over the quinoa, distributing it evenly between the two bowls.
6. Drizzle a tablespoon of almond butter over each bowl, adding a creamy, protein-rich element to the dish.
7. Sprinkle chia seeds on top for an added boost of fiber and omega-3 fatty acids.
8. If desired, add a drizzle of honey or maple syrup for a touch of natural sweetness.
9. Enjoy the Warm Pecan and Apple Breakfast Bowl as a hearty, nourishing start to your day, with the cozy flavors of cinnamon and nutmeg embracing you in comfort.

Nutritional Data:

Calories: 450 | Protein: 10g | Carbs: 40g (without optional sweeteners) | Fat: 30g | Fiber: 9g | Sugar: 15g (without optional sweeteners)

The Verdant Gardens of Crisp Delights

Esteemed reader, as we gracefully navigate the enriching contours of "The Galveston Diet for Beginners," we now step into the lush, verdant gardens where the artistry of salads awaits. This chapter is not just a sequence of recipes but a journey into a realm where the earth's bountiful harvest merges with the culinary poetry, each dish a harmonious ensemble of colors, textures, and flavors.

I am honored to be your companion in this green sanctuary, where every leaf, vegetable, and garnish is a note in a lyrical composition that sings the ballads of wellness and vitality, rooted in the guiding principles of the Galveston diet.

A Palette of Nature's Bounty
Imagine a world where the crunch of fresh vegetables, the burst of succulent fruits, and the whisper of fine herbs converge in a canvas of culinary artistry. Each salad is a palette of nature's bounty, a visual and sensory sonnet where the freshness of ingredients resonates with the richness of flavors.

Rooted in Galveston's Wisdom
With the foundational wisdom of the Galveston diet as our anchor, each salad is a garden of nutritional abundance. This chapter is where the crisp, refreshing textures and flavors of nature's offerings are tenderly adorned with dressings and accents that not only elevate the sensory experience but align with our journey toward holistic well-being.

The Dance of Seasons
In the unfolding narrative of salads, witness the dance of seasons where spring's tender blossoms, summer's vibrant fruits, autumn's earthy hues, and winter's robust harvest converge. Each recipe is a celebration of the seasons, a harmonious alignment of the earth's cycles, and the Galveston diet's nutritional ethos.

The Green Odyssey Awaits
Are you prepared, dear reader, to embark upon a green odyssey where salads are not just side dishes but main attractions, each a choreographed ballet of the earth's fresh offerings and the Galveston diet's nutritional grace?

Let's go!

Crisp Greens & Grilled Chicken Fusion

Preparation Time: 15 minutes | Cooking Time: 15 minutes | Portion Size: 4 servings

Ingredients:

For the Grilled Chicken:

- 4 boneless, skinless chicken breasts (about 4 ounces each)
- 2 tablespoons olive oil
- 2 cloves garlic, minced
- 1 teaspoon paprika
- Salt and pepper to taste

For the Salad:

- 8 cups mixed greens (such as spinach, kale, and arugula)
- 1 cup cherry tomatoes, halved
- 1 cucumber, thinly sliced
- 1/4 red onion, thinly sliced
- 1/4 cup Kalamata olives, pitted
- 1/4 cup crumbled feta cheese (optional)

For the Vinaigrette:

- 2 tablespoons extra-virgin olive oil
- 1 tablespoon red wine vinegar
- 1 teaspoon Dijon mustard
- Salt and pepper to taste

Instructions:

For the Grilled Chicken:

1. Preheat your grill or grill pan to medium-high heat.
2. In a small bowl, combine olive oil, minced garlic, paprika, salt, and pepper to create a marinade.
3. Brush the marinade over both sides of each chicken breast.
4. Grill the chicken breasts for about 6-7 minutes per side, or until they are cooked through and have nice grill marks. The internal temperature should reach 165°F (74°C).
5. Remove the chicken from the grill and let it rest for a few minutes before slicing.

For the Salad:

1. In a large salad bowl, combine the mixed greens, halved cherry tomatoes, thinly sliced cucumber, thinly sliced red onion, Kalamata olives, and crumbled feta cheese (if desired).

For the Vinaigrette:

1. In a small bowl, whisk together extra-virgin olive oil, red wine vinegar, Dijon mustard, salt, and pepper to create a vinaigrette.

To Serve:

1. Divide the salad among four plates.
2. Top each salad with sliced grilled chicken.
3. Drizzle the prepared vinaigrette over each salad.

Nutritional Data (per serving):

Calories: 290 | Carbohydrates: 8g | Protein: 30g | Fats: 16g | Fiber: 2g | Sugar: 3g

Zesty Lemon Shrimp Avocado Salad

Preparation Time: 15 minutes | Cooking Time: 5 minutes | Portion Size: 2 servings

Ingredients:

For the Lemon Shrimp:

- 10-12 large shrimp, peeled and deveined
- 1 tablespoon olive oil
- Zest of 1 lemon
- Juice of 1 lemon
- 2 cloves garlic, minced
- Salt and pepper to taste
- Crushed red pepper flakes (optional, for extra heat)

For the Salad:

- 4 cups mixed greens (such as spinach, arugula, and romaine)
- 1 ripe avocado, sliced
- 1/2 cup cherry tomatoes, halved
- 1/4 red onion, thinly sliced
- Fresh parsley leaves, chopped (for garnish, optional)

For the Vinaigrette:

- 2 tablespoons extra-virgin olive oil
- Juice of 1 lemon
- 1 teaspoon Dijon mustard
- Salt and pepper to taste

Instructions:

For the Lemon Shrimp:

1. In a bowl, combine the olive oil, lemon zest, lemon juice, minced garlic, salt, pepper, and optional crushed red pepper flakes.
2. Add the peeled and deveined shrimp to the bowl and toss to coat them in the marinade. Allow them to marinate for a few minutes while you prepare the rest of the salad.
3. Heat a skillet over medium-high heat. Once hot, add the marinated shrimp.
4. Cook the shrimp for about 2-3 minutes per side, or until they turn pink and opaque. Be careful not to overcook them. Remove from heat.

For the Salad:

1. In a large salad bowl, combine the mixed greens, sliced avocado, halved cherry tomatoes, and thinly sliced red onion.

For the Vinaigrette:

1. In a small bowl, whisk together the extra-virgin olive oil, lemon juice, Dijon mustard, salt, and pepper to create a vinaigrette.

To Serve:

1. Divide the salad mixture between two plates.
2. Top each salad with the zesty lemon shrimp.
3. Drizzle the prepared vinaigrette over each salad.
4. Garnish with chopped fresh parsley leaves if desired.

Nutritional Data (per serving):

Calories: 320 | Carbohydrates: 16g | Protein: 12g | Fats: 24g | Fiber: 9g | Sugar: 3g

Sesame-Ginger Salmon Salad Delight

Preparation Time: 15 minutes | Cooking Time: 10 minutes | Portion Size: 2 servings

Ingredients:

For the Sesame-Ginger Salmon:

- 2 salmon fillets (about 6 ounces each)
- 1 tablespoon sesame oil
- 1 tablespoon soy sauce (low-sodium)
- 1 teaspoon fresh ginger, minced
- 1 clove garlic, minced
- Salt and pepper to taste

For the Salad:

- 4 cups mixed greens (such as baby spinach, kale, and lettuce)
- 1 cup cucumber, thinly sliced
- 1/2 red bell pepper, thinly sliced
- 1/4 cup shredded carrots

- 2 green onions, thinly sliced
- 2 tablespoons sesame seeds (for garnish, optional)

For the Sesame-Ginger Dressing:

- 2 tablespoons sesame oil
- 1 tablespoon rice vinegar
- 1 teaspoon low-sodium soy sauce
- 1 teaspoon honey or a sugar substitute
- 1/2 teaspoon fresh ginger, minced
- Salt and pepper to taste

Instructions:

For the Sesame-Ginger Salmon:

1. In a bowl, whisk together sesame oil, soy sauce, minced ginger, minced garlic, salt, and pepper to create a marinade.
2. Place the salmon fillets in a shallow dish and pour the marinade over them. Let them marinate for about 10 minutes.
3. Heat a skillet over medium-high heat. Once hot, add the salmon fillets, skin-side down, and cook for approximately 3-4 minutes on each side, or until the salmon flakes easily with a fork. Remove from heat.
4. Once cooked, remove the skin from the salmon fillets, if desired, and flake the salmon into bite-sized pieces.

For the Salad:

1. In a large salad bowl, combine the mixed greens, thinly sliced cucumber, thinly sliced red bell pepper, shredded carrots, and sliced green onions.

For the Sesame-Ginger Dressing:

1. In a small bowl, whisk together sesame oil, rice vinegar, low-sodium soy sauce, honey (or sugar substitute), minced ginger, salt, and pepper to create the dressing.

To Serve:

Divide the salad mixture between two plates.

1. Top each salad with the flaked sesame-ginger salmon.
2. Drizzle the prepared sesame-ginger dressing over each salad.
3. Optionally, garnish with sesame seeds.

Nutritional Data (per serving):

Calories: 380 | Carbohydrates: 12g | Protein: 32g | Fats: 24g | Fiber: 3g | Sugar: 5g

---

Spiced Beef & Fresh Veggie Toss

Preparation Time: 15 minutes | Cooking Time: 10 minutes | Portion Size: 4 servings

Ingredients:

For the Spiced Beef:

- 1 pound lean ground beef
- 1 teaspoon ground cumin
- 1 teaspoon chili powder
- 1/2 teaspoon paprika
- Salt and pepper to taste

For the Fresh Veggie Toss:

- 2 cups mixed bell peppers, thinly sliced (assorted colors)
- 1 cup zucchini, thinly sliced
- 1 cup cherry tomatoes, halved
- 1/2 red onion, thinly sliced
- 2 cloves garlic, minced
- 2 tablespoons fresh cilantro, chopped (for garnish, optional)

For the Lime-Cilantro Dressing:

- Juice of 2 limes
- 2 tablespoons extra-virgin olive oil
- 1 teaspoon honey or a sugar substitute
- 1/4 cup fresh cilantro, chopped
- Salt and pepper to taste

Instructions:

For the Spiced Beef:

1. In a large skillet over medium-high heat, cook the lean ground beef until browned, breaking it apart as it cooks.
2. Drain any excess fat from the skillet.
3. Sprinkle the ground cumin, chili powder, paprika, salt, and pepper over the cooked beef. Stir well to evenly coat the beef with the spices. Cook for an additional 2-3 minutes. Remove from heat.

For the Fresh Veggie Toss:

1. In a large salad bowl, combine the thinly sliced mixed bell peppers, thinly sliced zucchini, halved cherry tomatoes, thinly sliced red onion, and minced garlic.

For the Lime-Cilantro Dressing:

1. In a small bowl, whisk together the lime juice, extra-virgin olive oil, honey (or sugar substitute), chopped fresh cilantro, salt, and pepper to create the dressing.

To Serve:

1. Divide the fresh veggie toss among four plates.
2. Top each plate with the spiced beef.
3. Drizzle the prepared lime-cilantro dressing over each serving.
4. Optionally, garnish with additional fresh cilantro.

Nutritional Data (per serving):

Calories: 280 | Carbohydrates: 14g | Protein: 20g | Fats: 16g | Fiber: 4g | Sugar: 7g

---

Sweet & Spicy Grilled Chicken Salad

Preparation Time: 20 minutes | Cooking Time: 15 minutes | Portion Size: 4 servings

Ingredients:

For the Sweet & Spicy Grilled Chicken:

- 4 boneless, skinless chicken breasts
- 2 tablespoons olive oil
- 1/4 cup honey
- 2 tablespoons Dijon mustard
- 1 teaspoon chili powder
- 1/2 teaspoon paprika
- Salt and pepper to taste

For the Salad:

- 8 cups mixed salad greens (such as romaine, spinach, and arugula)
- 1 cup cherry tomatoes, halved
- 1/2 cucumber, thinly sliced
- 1/4 red onion, thinly sliced
- 1/4 cup sliced almonds (for garnish, optional)

For the Balsamic Vinaigrette:

- 1/4 cup balsamic vinegar
- 1/4 cup extra-virgin olive oil
- 1 tablespoon honey or a sugar substitute
- Salt and pepper to taste

Instructions:

For the Sweet & Spicy Grilled Chicken:

1. Preheat your grill to medium-high heat.
2. In a small bowl, whisk together olive oil, honey, Dijon mustard, chili powder, paprika, salt, and pepper to create the marinade.
3. Place the chicken breasts in a resealable plastic bag and pour the marinade over them. Seal the bag and massage the marinade into the chicken. Let it marinate for about 10 minutes.
4. Grill the chicken for approximately 6-7 minutes on each side, or until the internal temperature reaches 165°F (75°C) and the chicken is cooked through. Remove from heat and let it rest for a few minutes before slicing.

For the Salad:

1. In a large salad bowl, combine the mixed salad greens, halved cherry tomatoes, thinly sliced cucumber, and thinly sliced red onion.

For the Balsamic Vinaigrette:

1. In a small bowl, whisk together balsamic vinegar, extra-virgin olive oil, honey (or sugar substitute), salt, and pepper to create the dressing.

To Serve:

1. Divide the salad mixture among four plates.
2. Top each salad with slices of the sweet & spicy grilled chicken.
3. Drizzle the prepared balsamic vinaigrette over each serving.
4. Optionally, garnish with sliced almonds for added crunch.

Nutritional Data (per serving):

Calories: 350 | Carbohydrates: 23g | Protein: 25g | Fats: 18g | Fiber: 3g | Sugar: 18g

Lively Lime & Tuna Salad Bowl

Preparation Time: 15 minutes | Cooking Time: 0 minutes | Portion Size: 2 servings

Ingredients:

For the Lively Lime & Tuna Salad:

- 2 cans (5 ounces each) of water-packed tuna, drained
- 1/2 red bell pepper, diced
- 1/2 yellow bell pepper, diced
- 1/4 red onion, finely chopped
- 1/4 cup fresh cilantro, chopped
- 2 tablespoons fresh lime juice
- 2 tablespoons extra-virgin olive oil
- Salt and pepper to taste

For the Salad Base:

- 4 cups mixed salad greens (such as spinach, arugula, and baby kale)

Instructions:

For the Lively Lime & Tuna Salad:

1. In a large mixing bowl, combine the drained tuna, diced red bell pepper, diced yellow bell pepper, finely chopped red onion, and fresh cilantro.
2. In a small bowl, whisk together the fresh lime juice and extra-virgin olive oil. Season with salt and pepper to taste.
3. Drizzle the lime and olive oil dressing over the tuna and vegetable mixture. Gently toss to coat everything evenly.

For the Salad Base:

1. Divide the mixed salad greens among two salad bowls, creating a base for your salad.

To Serve:

1. Spoon the Lively Lime & Tuna Salad mixture over the bed of salad greens in each bowl.
2. Garnish with additional cilantro if desired.

Nutritional Data (per serving):

Calories: 280 | Carbohydrates: 12g | Protein: 28g | Fats: 14g | Fiber: 4g | Sugar: 4g

---

Herb-Kissed Quinoa & Veggie Mix

Preparation Time: 15 minutes | Cooking Time: 20 minutes | Portion Size: 4 servings

Ingredients:

For the Quinoa & Veggie Mix:

- 1 cup quinoa, rinsed and drained
- 2 cups low-sodium vegetable broth
- 1 cup cherry tomatoes, halved
- 1 cup cucumber, diced
- 1/2 cup red bell pepper, diced
- 1/2 cup yellow bell pepper, diced
- 1/4 cup red onion, finely chopped
- 2 tablespoons fresh parsley, chopped
- 1 tablespoon fresh dill, chopped

For the Lemon-Herb Dressing:

- 2 tablespoons extra-virgin olive oil
- 2 tablespoons fresh lemon juice
- 1 clove garlic, minced
- Salt and pepper to taste

Instructions:

For the Quinoa & Veggie Mix:

1. In a medium saucepan, combine the rinsed quinoa and low-sodium vegetable broth. Bring to a boil, then reduce the heat to low, cover, and simmer for about 15-20 minutes, or until the quinoa is cooked and the liquid is absorbed. Remove from heat and let it cool.
2. In a large mixing bowl, combine the cooked quinoa, cherry tomatoes, diced cucumber, diced red bell pepper, diced yellow bell pepper, finely chopped red onion, fresh parsley, and fresh dill.

For the Lemon-Herb Dressing:

1. In a small bowl, whisk together the extra-virgin olive oil, fresh lemon juice, minced garlic, salt, and pepper to create the dressing.

To Serve:

1. Drizzle the Lemon-Herb Dressing over the quinoa and veggie mixture. Gently toss to coat everything evenly.
2. Serve at room temperature or chilled.

Nutritional Data (per serving):

Calories: 270 | Carbohydrates: 39g | Protein: 7g | Fats: 10g | Fiber: 5g | Sugar: 4g

---

Refreshing Citrus & Avocado Greens

Preparation Time: 15 minutes | Cooking Time: 0 minutes | Portion Size: 2 servings

Ingredients:

For the Citrus & Avocado Greens:

- 4 cups mixed salad greens (such as spinach, arugula, and baby kale)
- 1 avocado, sliced
- 1 orange, peeled and segmented
- 1 grapefruit, peeled and segmented

For the Zesty Citrus Dressing:

- 2 tablespoons extra-virgin olive oil
- 2 tablespoons fresh lemon juice
- 1 tablespoon fresh lime juice
- 1 teaspoon honey (optional)
- Salt and pepper to taste

Instructions:

For the Citrus & Avocado Greens:

1. In a large salad bowl, combine the mixed salad greens.
2. Add the sliced avocado, orange segments, and grapefruit segments to the salad greens.

For the Zesty Citrus Dressing:

1. In a small bowl, whisk together the extra-virgin olive oil, fresh lemon juice, fresh lime juice, and honey (if using). Season with salt and pepper to taste.

To Serve:

1. Drizzle the Zesty Citrus Dressing over the salad.
2. Gently toss the salad to evenly coat the greens and fruits with the dressing.

Nutritional Data (per serving):

Calories: 250 | Carbohydrates: 25g | Protein: 3g | Fats: 18g | Fiber: 8g | Sugar: 13g

---

Spicy Southwest Shrimp Salad

Preparation Time: 20 minutes | Cooking Time: 5 minutes | Portion Size: 2 servings

Ingredients:

For the Spicy Southwest Shrimp:

- 12 large shrimp, peeled and deveined
- 1 teaspoon chili powder
- 1/2 teaspoon cumin
- 1/2 teaspoon paprika
- 1/4 teaspoon cayenne pepper (adjust to taste)
- Salt and pepper to taste
- 1 tablespoon olive oil

For the Salad:

- 4 cups mixed salad greens (such as romaine, spinach, and iceberg)
- 1/2 cup black beans, drained and rinsed
- 1/2 cup corn kernels (fresh, frozen, or canned)
- 1/2 cup cherry tomatoes, halved
- 1/4 cup red onion, thinly sliced
- 1/4 cup fresh cilantro, chopped

For the Creamy Avocado Dressing:

- 1 ripe avocado
- 1/4 cup Greek yogurt
- 2 tablespoons lime juice
- 2 tablespoons water
- 1 clove garlic, minced
- Salt and pepper to taste

Instructions:

For the Spicy Southwest Shrimp:

1. In a small bowl, combine the chili powder, cumin, paprika, cayenne pepper, salt, and pepper.
2. Toss the peeled and deveined shrimp in the spice mixture until they are well coated.
3. In a skillet over medium-high heat, heat the olive oil. Add the seasoned shrimp and cook for about 2-3 minutes per side, or until they turn pink and opaque. Remove from heat and set aside.

For the Creamy Avocado Dressing:

1. In a blender or food processor, combine the ripe avocado, Greek yogurt, lime juice, water, minced garlic, salt, and pepper. Blend until smooth and creamy.

To Assemble the Salad:

1. In a large salad bowl, arrange the mixed salad greens as the base.
2. Top with black beans, corn kernels, cherry tomatoes, thinly sliced red onion, and fresh cilantro.
3. Place the spicy Southwest shrimp on top of the salad.
4. Drizzle the creamy avocado dressing over the salad.

Nutritional Data (per serving):

Calories: 360 | Carbohydrates: 29g | Protein: 23g | Fats: 20g | Fiber: 10g | Sugar: 4g

Mediterranean Chicken & Feta Greens

Preparation Time: 15 minutes | Cooking Time: 20 minutes | Portion Size: 2 servings

Ingredients:

For the Mediterranean Chicken:

- 2 boneless, skinless chicken breasts
- 1 tablespoon olive oil
- 1 teaspoon dried oregano
- 1 teaspoon dried basil
- 1/2 teaspoon garlic powder
- Salt and pepper to taste

For the Salad:

- 4 cups mixed salad greens (such as romaine, spinach, and arugula)
- 1/2 cup cherry tomatoes, halved
- 1/4 cup Kalamata olives, pitted and sliced
- 1/4 cup red onion, thinly sliced
- 1/4 cup crumbled feta cheese
- 2 tablespoons fresh parsley, chopped

For the Balsamic Vinaigrette:

- 2 tablespoons balsamic vinegar
- 1/4 cup extra-virgin olive oil
- 1 teaspoon Dijon mustard
- 1 teaspoon honey (optional)
- Salt and pepper to taste

Instructions:

For the Mediterranean Chicken:

1. In a small bowl, combine the dried oregano, dried basil, garlic powder, salt, and pepper.
2. Rub the spice mixture evenly over both sides of the chicken breasts.
3. In a skillet over medium-high heat, heat the olive oil. Add the seasoned chicken breasts and cook for about 6-7 minutes per side, or until they are cooked through and no longer pink in the center. Remove from heat and let them rest for a few minutes before slicing.

For the Balsamic Vinaigrette:

1. In a small bowl, whisk together the balsamic vinegar, extra-virgin olive oil, Dijon mustard, honey (if using), salt, and pepper until well combined.

To Assemble the Salad:

1. In a large salad bowl, arrange the mixed salad greens as the base.
2. Top with cherry tomatoes, Kalamata olives, thinly sliced red onion, crumbled feta cheese, and fresh parsley.
3. Slice the cooked Mediterranean chicken and place it on top of the salad.
4. Drizzle the balsamic vinaigrette over the salad.

Nutritional Data (per serving):

Calories: 400 | Carbohydrates: 12g | Protein: 28g | Fats: 28g | Fiber: 4g | Sugar: 5g

Tangy Lemon Herb Steak Salad

Preparation Time: 15 minutes | Cooking Time: 10 minutes | Portion Size: 2 servings

Ingredients:

For the Lemon Herb Steak:

- 1 pound flank steak
- 1 tablespoon olive oil
- Zest and juice of 1 lemon
- 2 cloves garlic, minced
- 1 teaspoon dried oregano
- 1 teaspoon dried thyme
- Salt and pepper to taste

For the Salad:

- 6 cups mixed salad greens (e.g., arugula, spinach, and romaine)
- 1 cup cherry tomatoes, halved
- 1/2 cucumber, thinly sliced
- 1/4 red onion, thinly sliced
- 1/4 cup feta cheese, crumbled
- 2 tablespoons fresh parsley, chopped

For the Lemon Herb Dressing:

- 2 tablespoons olive oil
- Zest and juice of 1 lemon
- 1 teaspoon Dijon mustard
- 1 teaspoon honey (optional)
- Salt and pepper to taste

Instructions:

For the Lemon Herb Steak:

1. In a small bowl, whisk together the olive oil, lemon zest, lemon juice, minced garlic, dried oregano, dried thyme, salt, and pepper.
2. Place the flank steak in a shallow dish and pour the marinade over it. Make sure the steak is well-coated. Let it marinate for at least 15 minutes, or longer if time allows.
3. Preheat a grill or grill pan over medium-high heat. Grill the marinated steak for about 4-5 minutes per side for medium-rare, or longer to your desired level of doneness. Remove the steak from the grill and let it rest for a few minutes before slicing.

For the Lemon Herb Dressing:

1. In a small bowl, whisk together the olive oil, lemon zest, lemon juice, Dijon mustard, honey (if using), salt, and pepper until well combined.

To Assemble the Salad:

1. In a large salad bowl, arrange the mixed salad greens as the base.
2. Top with halved cherry tomatoes, sliced cucumber, thinly sliced red onion, crumbled feta cheese, and fresh parsley.
3. Slice the grilled lemon herb steak and place it on top of the salad.
4. Drizzle the lemon herb dressing over the salad.

Nutritional Data (per serving):

Calories: 400 | Carbohydrates: 12g | Protein: 32g | Fats: 26g | Fiber: 4g | Sugar: 5g

Sweet Beet & Goat Cheese Harmony

Preparation Time: 15 minutes | Cooking Time: 45 minutes | Portion Size: 2 servings

Ingredients:

For the Roasted Beets:

- 2 medium-sized beets, trimmed and peeled
- 1 tablespoon olive oil
- Salt and pepper to taste

For the Goat Cheese Dressing:

- 2 tablespoons goat cheese, crumbled
- 2 tablespoons plain Greek yogurt
- 1 tablespoon olive oil
- 1 tablespoon fresh lemon juice
- 1 clove garlic, minced
- Salt and pepper to taste

For the Salad:

- 4 cups mixed salad greens (e.g., baby spinach, arugula, and leafy lettuce)
- 1/4 cup pecans, toasted and chopped
- 1/4 cup fresh basil leaves, torn
- 2 tablespoons red onion, thinly sliced

Instructions:

For the Roasted Beets:

1. Preheat your oven to 400°F (200°C).
2. Cut the peeled and trimmed beets into small wedges or cubes.
3. Place the beet pieces on a baking sheet, drizzle with olive oil, and season with salt and pepper. Toss to coat evenly.
4. Roast the beets in the preheated oven for about 40-45 minutes or until they are tender when pierced with a fork. Remove from the oven and let them cool slightly.

For the Goat Cheese Dressing:

1. In a small bowl, combine the crumbled goat cheese, plain Greek yogurt, olive oil, fresh lemon juice, minced garlic, salt, and pepper.

Whisk until the dressing is smooth and well mixed.

To Assemble the Salad:

1. In a large salad bowl, arrange the mixed salad greens as the base.
2. Top the greens with the roasted beet pieces, toasted and chopped pecans, torn fresh basil leaves, and thinly sliced red onion.
3. Drizzle the goat cheese dressing over the salad.

Nutritional Data (per serving):

Calories: 320 | Carbohydrates: 20g | Protein: 8g | Fats: 25g | Fiber: 6g | Sugar: 9g

Crunchy Kale & Roasted Veg Medley

Preparation Time: 15 minutes | Cooking Time: 25 minutes | Portion Size: 2 servings

Ingredients:

For the Roasted Vegetables:

- 1 cup sweet potatoes, peeled and diced
- 1 cup red bell pepper, sliced
- 1 cup zucchini, sliced
- 1 tablespoon olive oil
- Salt and pepper to taste
- 1/2 teaspoon paprika (optional)

For the Kale Salad:

- 4 cups kale leaves, stems removed and chopped
- 1 tablespoon olive oil
- 1 tablespoon fresh lemon juice
- 1/4 cup cherry tomatoes, halved
- 1/4 cup cucumber, sliced
- 2 tablespoons red onion, thinly sliced
- 2 tablespoons pumpkin seeds (pepitas), toasted
- 2 tablespoons crumbled feta cheese (optional)

Instructions:

For the Roasted Vegetables:

1. Preheat your oven to 400°F (200°C).
2. In a large mixing bowl, combine the diced sweet potatoes, sliced red bell pepper, and sliced zucchini.
3. Drizzle olive oil over the vegetables and season with salt, pepper, and paprika (if using). Toss to coat the vegetables evenly.
4. Spread the vegetables in a single layer on a baking sheet.
5. Roast in the preheated oven for approximately 20-25 minutes or until the vegetables are tender and slightly caramelized. Stir occasionally for even cooking.

For the Kale Salad:

1. While the vegetables are roasting, place the chopped kale in a large salad bowl.
2. Drizzle olive oil and fresh lemon juice over the kale. Massage the kale leaves gently for a few minutes until they become tender and well-coated with the dressing.
3. Add the halved cherry tomatoes, sliced cucumber, and thinly sliced red onion to the kale. Toss to combine.

To Assemble the Medley:

1. Once the roasted vegetables are done, let them cool slightly.
2. Add the roasted vegetables to the kale salad.
3. Sprinkle toasted pumpkin seeds and crumbled feta cheese (if using) over the top.

Nutritional Data (per serving):

Calories: 330 | Carbohydrates: 38g | Protein: 8g | Fats: 18g | Fiber: 7g | Sugar: 9g

Tropical Mango & Grilled Fish Bliss

Preparation Time: 15 minutes | Cooking Time: 10 minutes | Portion Size: 2 servings

Ingredients:

For the Grilled Fish:

- 2 white fish fillets (such as tilapia or snapper), about 6 oz each
- 1 tablespoon olive oil
- 1 teaspoon paprika
- Salt and pepper to taste
- 1 lime, cut into wedges for serving

For the Mango Salsa:

- 1 ripe mango, peeled, pitted, and diced
- 1/4 cup red bell pepper, finely diced
- 2 tablespoons red onion, finely chopped
- 1 small jalapeño pepper, seeded and finely chopped (adjust to your desired level of spiciness)
- 2 tablespoons fresh cilantro, chopped
- Juice of 1 lime
- Salt to taste

Instructions:

For the Grilled Fish:

1. Preheat your grill to medium-high heat.
2. In a small bowl, combine olive oil, paprika, salt, and pepper.
3. Brush the fish fillets with the olive oil mixture on both sides.
4. Place the fish fillets on the grill and cook for about 4-5 minutes per side or until they are opaque and easily flake with a fork.
5. Remove the grilled fish from the heat and squeeze fresh lime juice over them.

For the Mango Salsa:

1. In a separate bowl, combine the diced mango, red bell pepper, red onion, jalapeño pepper, and fresh cilantro.

2. Squeeze the juice of one lime over the mixture and add a pinch of salt. Toss everything together until well combined.

To Serve:

1. Place a grilled fish fillet on each serving plate.
2. Top the fish with a generous portion of the tropical mango salsa.

Nutritional Data (per serving):

Calories: 275 | Carbohydrates: 29g | Protein: 28g | Fats: 7g | Fiber: 4g | Sugar: 22g

Classic Caesar with a Grilled Chicken Twist

Preparation Time: 20 minutes | Cooking Time: 15 minutes | Portion Size: 2 servings

Ingredients:

For the Grilled Chicken:

- 2 boneless, skinless chicken breasts
- 1 tablespoon olive oil
- 1 teaspoon dried Italian seasoning
- Salt and pepper to taste

For the Caesar Salad:

- 1 head of Romaine lettuce, washed and chopped
- 1/4 cup grated Parmesan cheese
- 1/2 cup Vegan Caesar dressing
- 1/2 cup croutons (optional, choose whole-grain or gluten-free if desired)
- Lemon wedges for serving (optional)

Instructions:

For the Grilled Chicken:

1. Preheat your grill to medium-high heat.
2. Brush the chicken breasts with olive oil and sprinkle them with dried Italian seasoning, salt, and pepper.

3. Place the chicken breasts on the grill and cook for about 6-7 minutes per side or until they reach an internal temperature of 165°F (74°C) and have grill marks.

4. Remove the grilled chicken from the heat and let them rest for a few minutes before slicing.

For the Caesar Salad:

1. In a large salad bowl, combine the chopped Romaine lettuce and grated Parmesan cheese.

2. Drizzle the Caesar dressing over the lettuce and cheese. Toss everything together until the lettuce is well coated with the dressing.

To Serve:

1. Divide the Caesar salad between two plates.

2. Slice the grilled chicken breasts and place them on top of each salad.

3. If desired, add croutons for extra crunch and serve with lemon wedges for a burst of fresh flavor.

Nutritional Data (per serving, without croutons):

Calories: 360 | Carbohydrates: 9g | Protein: 30g | Fats: 23g | Fiber: 2g | Sugar: 2g

Asian-Inspired Beef & Broccoli Salad

Preparation Time: 15 minutes | Cooking Time: 10 minutes | Portion Size: 2 servings

Ingredients:

For the Beef and Broccoli:

- 8 oz (225g) flank steak, thinly sliced
- 2 cups broccoli florets
- 1 tablespoon olive oil
- 2 cloves garlic, minced
- 1 teaspoon fresh ginger, minced
- Salt and pepper to taste

For the Salad:

- 4 cups mixed salad greens (e.g., spinach, kale, arugula)
- 1/2 cucumber, thinly sliced
- 1 carrot, julienned
- 1/4 red bell pepper, thinly sliced
- 2 green onions, thinly sliced

For the Dressing:

- 2 tablespoons reduced-sodium soy sauce
- 1 tablespoon rice vinegar
- 1 tablespoon sesame oil
- 1 teaspoon honey (adjust to taste)
- 1 teaspoon sesame seeds (for garnish, optional)

Instructions:

For the Beef and Broccoli:

1. In a large skillet or wok, heat the olive oil over medium-high heat.
2. Add the minced garlic and ginger to the skillet and sauté for about 30 seconds or until fragrant.
3. Add the thinly sliced flank steak to the skillet. Season with salt and pepper. Stir-fry for 2-3 minutes or until the beef is browned and cooked to your desired level of doneness. Remove the beef from the skillet and set it aside.
4. In the same skillet, add the broccoli florets. Cook for 3-4 minutes, stirring frequently until the broccoli is tender but still crisp.
5. Return the cooked beef to the skillet with the broccoli and stir to combine. Remove from heat.

For the Salad:

1. In a large salad bowl, combine the mixed salad greens, thinly sliced cucumber, julienned carrot, red bell pepper slices, and green onions.

For the Dressing:

1. In a small bowl, whisk together the reduced-sodium soy sauce, rice vinegar, sesame oil, and honey until well combined.

To Serve:

1. Divide the salad mixture between two plates.
2. Top each salad with the beef and broccoli mixture.
3. Drizzle the dressing over the salad and beef.
4. If desired, sprinkle with sesame seeds for garnish.

Nutritional Data (per serving):

Calories: 340 | Carbohydrates: 16g | Protein: 27g | Fats: 19g | Fiber: 5g | Sugar: 6g

Roasted Veg & Quinoa Power Bowl

Preparation Time: 15 minutes | Cooking Time: 25 minutes | Portion Size: 2 servings

Ingredients:

For the Roasted Vegetables:

- 1 cup sweet potatoes, cubed
- 1 cup bell peppers, sliced
- 1 cup zucchini, sliced
- 1 cup cherry tomatoes
- 2 tablespoons olive oil
- Salt and pepper to taste
- 1/2 teaspoon dried thyme

For the Quinoa:

- 1/2 cup quinoa, rinsed and drained
- 1 cup water

For the Dressing:

- 2 tablespoons extra-virgin olive oil
- 1 tablespoon balsamic vinegar
- 1 clove garlic, minced
- Salt and pepper to taste

For Assembly:

- 2 cups mixed salad greens (e.g., spinach, kale, arugula)
- 1/4 cup feta cheese, crumbled (optional)
- 1 tablespoon pumpkin seeds (optional)

Instructions:

For the Roasted Vegetables:

1. Preheat your oven to 400°F (200°C).
2. In a large mixing bowl, combine the sweet potatoes, bell peppers, zucchini, cherry tomatoes, olive oil, salt, pepper, and dried thyme. Toss to coat the vegetables evenly.
3. Spread the seasoned vegetables on a baking sheet in a single layer.
4. Roast in the preheated oven for about 20-25 minutes or until the vegetables are tender and slightly caramelized, stirring once halfway through cooking. Remove from the oven and set aside.

For the Quinoa:

1. In a medium saucepan, combine the rinsed quinoa and water. Bring to a boil over high heat.
2. Once boiling, reduce the heat to low, cover, and simmer for about 15 minutes or until the quinoa is cooked and the liquid is absorbed. Fluff with a fork and set aside.

For the Dressing:

1. In a small bowl, whisk together the extra-virgin olive oil, balsamic vinegar, minced garlic, salt, and pepper until well combined.

To Assemble the Power Bowl:

1. Divide the mixed salad greens between two serving bowls.
2. Spoon the cooked quinoa over the greens in each bowl.
3. Top the quinoa with the roasted vegetables.
4. Drizzle the dressing over the roasted veg and quinoa.
5. If desired, sprinkle with crumbled feta cheese and pumpkin seeds for added flavor and texture.

Nutritional Data (per serving, without optional toppings):

Calories: 390 | Carbohydrates: 46g | Protein: 7g | Fats: 21g | Fiber: 8g | Sugar: 10g

---

Grilled Salmon & Asparagus Delight

Preparation Time: 15 minutes | Cooking Time: 15 minutes | Portion Size: 2 servings

Ingredients:

For the Grilled Salmon:

- 2 salmon fillets (6-8 ounces each)
- 1 tablespoon olive oil
- 1 teaspoon lemon zest
- 1 teaspoon lemon juice
- 1 teaspoon fresh dill, chopped
- Salt and pepper to taste

For the Grilled Asparagus:

- 1 bunch of asparagus spears, woody ends trimmed
- 1 tablespoon olive oil
- Salt and pepper to taste

For the Lemon Dill Sauce:

- 1/4 cup Greek yogurt
- 1 tablespoon fresh lemon juice
- 1 teaspoon lemon zest
- 1 teaspoon fresh dill, chopped
- Salt and pepper to taste

Instructions:

For the Grilled Salmon:

1. Preheat your grill to medium-high heat (about 400°F or 200°C).
2. In a small bowl, mix the olive oil, lemon zest, lemon juice, fresh dill, salt, and pepper to create a marinade.
3. Place the salmon fillets on a plate, skin side down. Brush the marinade generously over the salmon fillets.
4. Once the grill is hot, oil the grates to prevent sticking. Place the salmon fillets on the grill, skin side down.
5. Grill the salmon for about 4-6 minutes per side, or until the salmon flakes easily with a fork and has nice grill marks. Cooking time may vary depending on the thickness of the fillets.

For the Grilled Asparagus:

1. While the salmon is grilling, toss the trimmed asparagus spears with olive oil, salt, and pepper.
2. Place the asparagus directly on the grill and cook for about 4-5 minutes, turning occasionally, until they are tender and slightly charred.

For the Lemon Dill Sauce:

1. In a small bowl, combine Greek yogurt, fresh lemon juice, lemon zest, fresh dill, salt, and pepper. Mix well to make the sauce.

To Serve:

1. Divide the grilled salmon and asparagus evenly between two plates.
2. Drizzle the lemon dill sauce over the grilled salmon.

Nutritional Data (per serving):

Calories: 370 | Carbohydrates: 7g | Protein: 34g | Fats: 22g | Fiber: 3g | Sugar: 3g

Cajun-Spiced Chicken & Avocado Mix

Preparation Time: 15 minutes | Cooking Time: 15 minutes | Portion Size: 2 servings

Ingredients:

For the Cajun-Spiced Chicken:

- 2 boneless, skinless chicken breasts (6-8 ounces each)
- 1 tablespoon olive oil
- 1 tablespoon Cajun seasoning
- Salt and pepper to taste

For the Avocado Mix:

- 2 ripe avocados, diced
- 1 cup cherry tomatoes, halved
- 1/2 red onion, finely diced
- 1/4 cup fresh cilantro, chopped
- 1 lime, juiced
- Salt and pepper to taste

Instructions:

For the Cajun-Spiced Chicken:

1. In a small bowl, mix the Cajun seasoning with a pinch of salt and pepper.
2. Season the chicken breasts evenly on both sides with the Cajun seasoning mixture.
3. In a skillet, heat the olive oil over medium-high heat.
4. Add the seasoned chicken breasts to the skillet and cook for about 6-7 minutes per side, or until they reach an internal temperature of 165°F (74°C) and are no longer pink in the center. Cooking time may vary depending on the thickness of the chicken breasts.
5. Once cooked, remove the chicken from the skillet and let it rest for a few minutes before slicing.

For the Avocado Mix:

1. In a large bowl, combine the diced avocados, cherry tomatoes, finely diced red onion, chopped cilantro, and lime juice.
2. Season the mixture with salt and pepper to taste. Toss everything together gently.

To Serve:

1. Divide the Cajun-spiced chicken slices between two plates.
2. Top the chicken with the avocado mix, spreading it over and beside the chicken.

Nutritional Data (per serving):

Calories: 440 | Carbohydrates: 21g | Protein: 28g | Fats: 30g | Fiber: 11g | Sugar: 4g

A Journey into the Soulful World of Soups

Warm greetings once more, cherished reader. As we gracefully turn the pages of "The Galveston Diet for Beginners," we find ourselves enveloped in the comforting, soul-stirring world of soups. In this chapter, we don't just share recipes; we weave narratives of warmth, healing, and nourishment that every spoonful promises to deliver. Each bowl is a crafted harmony of ingredients, echoing the holistic ethos of the Galveston diet.

In the peaceful embrace of these pages, I'm delighted to extend my hand and invite you to a world where the simmering pot on the stove is not just about food. It's a vessel of aromas, flavors, and stories that nurtures the body and soul, a delightful refuge where every sip is a warm hug, ushering comfort, wellness, and joy.

The Art of Sipping Wellness

What makes a soup special? Is it the tender dance of ingredients, each bringing its unique essence to the bowl? Or the way every spoonful warms us from the inside, echoing the tender embrace of a loved one? In the world of the Galveston diet, soup is an artistic expression, a crafted balance of nutrients that supports our journey to radiant health.

Soup Alchemy

Each recipe encapsulates the meticulous alchemy of fresh, wholesome ingredients, underpinned by the scientific grounding of the Galveston diet. We will venture together through a myriad of flavors, from the rustic, hearty bowls that echo the warmth of a homely embrace to the light, invigorating broths that spring the soul to life.

Healing in Every Bowl

In this chapter, every recipe is a testament to the healing power of mindful nutrition. We delve into the essence of ingredients that are not only flavorful but imbued with benefits that align with the Galveston principles. Each soup is a healing journey, a delightful dance of aromas and tastes that nurture holistic well-being.

Let's Simmer Together!

Are you ready to immerse in the delightful escapade of sipping, tasting, and savoring? To stir the pot, where ingredients, affection, and science meld into concoctions of healing and pleasure? Your spoon is the key, unlocking a world where every sip is an embrace, every aroma a pathway to well-being, and every bowl a celebration of the Galveston diet's harmonious dance of flavors and health.

With a heart brimming with anticipation and warmth, I invite you to stir, sip, and savor. In the world of soups, we don't just feed the body; we nourish the soul, and together, we embark on a journey where each bowl is a heartfelt melody of taste, nutrition, and the tender, loving touch of the Galveston diet.

Velvety Tomato Basil Bliss

Preparation Time: 10 minutes | Cooking Time: 25 minutes | Portion Size: 4 servings

Ingredients:

- 8 ripe tomatoes, diced
- 1 small onion, chopped
- 3 cloves garlic, minced
- 2 cups vegetable broth, low sodium
- 1 tablespoon olive oil
- 1/2 cup fresh basil leaves, chopped
- 1 teaspoon sea salt
- 1/2 teaspoon black pepper
- 1/4 cup coconut cream

Instructions:

1. In a large saucepan, heat the olive oil over medium heat. Add the onions and cook until they are soft and translucent about 5 minutes.
2. Stir in the garlic and cook for an additional minute, until fragrant.
3. Add the diced tomatoes to the pan, stirring to combine with the onions and garlic. Cook for about 5-7 minutes until the tomatoes are soft.
4. Pour in the vegetable broth and bring the mixture to a gentle boil. Reduce the heat and let it simmer for 15 minutes.
5. Remove the saucepan from the heat and let it cool slightly. Then, using an immersion blender, puree the soup until smooth. You can also transfer the mixture to a traditional blender, but be sure to allow the steam to escape to prevent pressure build-up.
6. Return the pureed soup to low heat and stir in the chopped basil, sea salt, and pepper. Allow the flavors to meld together for an additional 5 minutes.
7. Just before serving, stir in the coconut cream to give the soup a creamy, velvety texture without adding dairy.
8. Serve hot, garnished with a sprig of fresh basil for a touch of color and aroma.

Nutritional Data:

Calories: 150 | Protein: 3g | Carbs: 16g | Fat: 9g | Fiber: 4g | Sugar: 9g

Spiced Pumpkin Harvest Soup

Preparation Time: 15 minutes | Cooking Time: 20 minutes | Portion Size: 4 servings

Ingredients:

- 2 cups pumpkin puree
- 1 large onion, chopped
- 3 cloves garlic, minced
- 2 cups vegetable broth, low sodium
- 1 cup coconut milk
- 1 tablespoon olive oil
- 1 teaspoon ground cinnamon
- 1/2 teaspoon ground nutmeg
- Salt and pepper to taste
- Fresh parsley for garnish (optional)

Instructions:

1. Heat the olive oil in a large pot over medium heat. Add the onions and cook until they are soft and translucent.
2. Add the garlic and continue to cook for another minute until the aroma of the garlic fills the air.
3. Pour in the vegetable broth and bring the mixture to a gentle simmer.
4. Stir in the pumpkin puree, blending it smoothly into the broth. Allow this mixture to cook for about 10 minutes.
5. Sprinkle in the cinnamon and nutmeg, stirring to distribute the spices evenly throughout the soup.
6. Pour in the coconut milk, blending it into the soup for a rich, creamy texture.
7. Allow the soup to simmer for an additional 10 minutes on low heat. Season with salt and pepper to taste.
8. Serve the soup hot, garnished with a sprig of fresh parsley if desired.

Nutritional Data:

Calories: 180 | Protein: 3g | Carbs: 19g | Fat: 12g | Fiber: 5g | Sugar: 8g

---

Creamy Cauliflower Comfort Bowl

Preparation Time: 10 minutes | Cooking Time: 20 minutes | Serves: 4

Ingredients:

- 1 large cauliflower, cut into florets
- 3 tablespoons olive oil
- 1 onion, finely chopped
- 2 garlic cloves, minced
- 4 cups vegetable broth, low sodium
- 1 teaspoon sea salt, adjust to taste
- 1/2 teaspoon black pepper, adjust to taste
- 1/4 teaspoon turmeric powder
- 1/4 cup almond milk, unsweetened
- 2 tablespoons fresh parsley, chopped (for garnish)

Instructions:

1. Heat the olive oil in a large pot over medium heat. Add the onions and garlic, sautéing until they become tender and fragrant.
2. Add the cauliflower florets to the pot and stir well to coat them in the oil and aromatics.
3. Pour the vegetable broth into the pot and bring the mixture to a boil. Reduce the heat and let it simmer for about 15-20 minutes, or until the cauliflower is tender.
4. Use an immersion blender or transfer the soup to a standard blender (in batches if necessary). Blend until smooth.
5. Return the blended soup to the pot (if using a standard blender), and stir in the sea salt, black pepper, and turmeric powder.
6. Add the almond milk and stir well to combine. Allow the soup to cook for an additional 5 minutes over low heat.
7. Serve hot, garnished with fresh parsley.

Nutritional Data:

Calories: 180 | Carbohydrates: 12g | Protein: 5g | Fats: 14g | Fiber: 5g | Sugar: 5g

---

Lemongrass Chicken Soup Zing

Preparation Time: 15 minutes | Cooking Time: 25 minutes | Serves: 4

Ingredients:

- 1 tablespoon coconut oil
- 2 chicken breasts, sliced into thin strips
- 1 stalk lemongrass, minced
- 3 cloves garlic, minced
- 1 small ginger root, grated
- 4 cups low-sodium chicken broth
- 1 cup coconut milk
- 2 tablespoons fish sauce
- 1 cup sliced mushrooms
- 1 red bell pepper, sliced
- 2 green onions, chopped
- Juice of 1 lime
- Fresh cilantro, for garnish
- Red chili flakes (optional)

Instructions:

1. Heat the coconut oil in a large pot over medium heat. Add the chicken strips and cook until they are browned and cooked through. Remove the chicken and set aside.
2. In the same pot, add the minced lemongrass, garlic, and grated ginger. Sauté until aromatic.
3. Pour the chicken broth and coconut milk into the pot. Bring the mixture to a simmer.
4. Return the cooked chicken to the pot and add fish sauce, stirring to combine.
5. Add the sliced mushrooms and red bell pepper to the soup. Let it simmer for another 10 minutes until the vegetables are tender.
6. Stir in the chopped green onions and lime juice. Adjust the seasoning with red chili flakes if desired, and simmer for an additional 5 minutes.
7. Serve the soup hot, garnished with fresh cilantro.

Nutritional Data:

Calories: 270 | Carbohydrates: 10g | Protein: 25g | Fats: 15g | Fiber: 2g | Sugar: 4g

Garlicky Greens & Bean Soup

Preparation Time: 10 minutes | Cooking Time: 20 minutes | Serves: 4

Ingredients:

- 1 tablespoon olive oil
- 4 cloves garlic, minced
- 1 onion, chopped
- 4 cups low-sodium vegetable broth
- 2 cans (15 ounces each) white beans, drained and rinsed
- 4 cups mixed greens (kale, spinach, swiss chard), chopped
- 1 teaspoon sea salt
- 1/2 teaspoon black pepper
- 1 tablespoon lemon juice

- Grated Parmesan cheese (optional, for garnish)
- Red pepper flakes (optional, for garnish)

Instructions:

1. Heat the olive oil in a large pot over medium heat. Add the minced garlic and chopped onion. Sauté until the onion is translucent and the garlic is fragrant.
2. Pour in the vegetable broth and increase the heat to bring the mixture to a boil.
3. Once boiling, add the drained and rinsed white beans. Reduce the heat and let the mixture simmer for about 10 minutes.
4. Add the mixed greens to the pot, stirring well to combine. Season with sea salt and black pepper.
5. Allow the soup to simmer for an additional 5-7 minutes, or until the greens are wilted and tender.
6. Remove the pot from the heat and stir in the lemon juice.
7. Serve the soup hot, optionally garnished with a sprinkle of grated Parmesan cheese and a pinch of red pepper flakes for an extra kick of flavor.

Nutritional Data:

Calories: 230 | Carbohydrates: 35g | Protein: 14g | Fats: 3g | Fiber: 9g | Sugar: 3g

Roasted Red Pepper Delight

Preparation Time: 15 minutes | Cooking Time: 25 minutes | Serves: 4

Ingredients:

- 4 red bell peppers
- 2 tablespoons olive oil
- 1 small onion, diced
- 3 cloves garlic, minced
- 4 cups low-sodium vegetable broth
- 1 teaspoon smoked paprika
- 1 teaspoon cumin
- Sea salt and black pepper to taste
- Fresh basil leaves for garnish

Instructions:

1. Preheat the oven to 400°F (200°C). Place the red peppers on a baking sheet and roast for about 20-25 minutes, or until the skins are charred and blistered. Remove from the oven and let them cool.
2. Once cool, peel off the skins and remove the stems and seeds. Chop the roasted peppers into chunks.
3. In a large pot, heat the olive oil over medium heat. Add the diced onion and minced garlic, sautéing until soft and fragrant.
4. Add the chopped roasted red peppers to the pot and stir well.
5. Pour in the vegetable broth and bring the mixture to a boil. Reduce the heat to low and let it simmer.
6. Add the smoked paprika, cumin, salt, and pepper. Stir well and let the soup simmer for another 10 minutes to allow the flavors to meld together.
7. Use an immersion blender to puree the soup until smooth, or transfer it to a blender in batches and blend until smooth.
8. Serve hot, garnished with fresh basil leaves.

Nutritional Data:

Calories: 140 | Carbohydrates: 18g | Protein: 3g | Fats: 7g | Fiber: 4g | Sugar: 10g

Turmeric Infused Chicken Broth

Preparation Time: 10 minutes | Cooking Time: 50 minutes | Serves: 6

Ingredients:

- 2 lbs. of chicken bones
- 1 large onion, roughly chopped
- 3 cloves of garlic, minced
- 2 carrots, chopped
- 2 celery stalks, chopped
- 1 tablespoon turmeric powder
- 1 teaspoon black pepper
- 2 bay leaves

- 8 cups of water
- Salt to taste
- Fresh parsley for garnish (optional)

Instructions:

1. In a large pot, combine the chicken bones, onion, garlic, carrots, and celery.
2. Add turmeric powder, black pepper, and bay leaves, mixing well to evenly coat the bones and vegetables.
3. Pour in 8 cups of water and bring the mixture to a boil over medium-high heat.
4. Once boiling, reduce the heat to low and let the broth simmer, covered, for about 45 minutes.
5. Strain the broth to remove the bones and vegetables, reserving the liquid.
6. Season the broth with salt to taste. Optionally, you can add more black pepper or turmeric to reach the desired flavor.
7. Serve the broth hot, garnished with fresh parsley if desired. The broth can also be stored in an airtight container in the refrigerator for up to 5 days or in the freezer for up to 3 months.

Nutritional Data:

Calories: 40 | Carbohydrates: 5g | Protein: 6g | Fats: 0.5g | Fiber: 1g | Sugar: 2g

Zesty Lime & Avocado Soup

Preparation Time: 15 minutes | Cooking Time: 0 minutes | Serves: 4

Ingredients:

- 3 ripe avocados, peeled and pitted
- 1/4 cup fresh lime juice
- 2 cups chicken or vegetable broth, chilled
- 1/2 cup coconut milk
- 1/2 teaspoon cayenne pepper
- Salt and black pepper, to taste
- 2 tablespoons chopped fresh cilantro
- 1 tomato, diced (for garnish)
- 2 tablespoons of red onion, finely chopped (for garnish)

Instructions:

1. In a blender or food processor, combine the avocados, lime juice, chilled broth, coconut milk, and cayenne pepper.
2. Blend until smooth, adjusting the consistency with additional broth if necessary. Season with salt and black pepper to taste.
3. Chill the soup for at least 30 minutes in the refrigerator before serving, to allow the flavors to meld together.
4. Divide the soup into four serving bowls.
5. Garnish with a sprinkle of fresh cilantro, diced tomato, and chopped red onion.
6. Serve immediately, and enjoy the refreshing, creamy, and zesty flavors dancing on your palate.

Note: This soup is served cold, making it a perfect refreshing meal for warmer days, rich in healthy fats and vibrant flavors.

Nutritional Data:

Calories: 270 | Carbohydrates: 15g | Protein: 4g | Fats: 24g | Fiber: 9g | Sugar: 3g

Ginger Spice Carrot Soup

Preparation Time: 15 minutes | Cooking Time: 25 minutes | Serves: 4

Ingredients:

- 1 tablespoon olive oil
- 1 onion, chopped
- 2 cloves garlic, minced
- 2 tablespoons grated fresh ginger
- 1 teaspoon ground turmeric
- 1/2 teaspoon ground cumin
- 1/4 teaspoon cayenne pepper (optional)
- 6 large carrots, peeled and sliced
- 4 cups low-sodium vegetable broth
- Salt and pepper to taste
- 1 can (13.5 ounces) coconut milk
- Fresh cilantro leaves, for garnish

Instructions:

1. In a large pot, heat the olive oil over medium heat. Add the onions and cook until they are soft and translucent about 5 minutes.
2. Stir in the garlic, ginger, turmeric, cumin, and cayenne pepper (if using), and cook for another 2 minutes until fragrant.
3. Add the sliced carrots to the pot and stir to coat with the spice mixture.
4. Pour in the vegetable broth and bring the mixture to a boil. Reduce the heat and let it simmer for about 20 minutes, or until the carrots are tender.
5. Use an immersion blender to puree the soup until smooth, or carefully transfer the soup to a regular blender in batches and puree.
6. Stir in the coconut milk and heat the soup for another 5 minutes. Season with salt and pepper to taste.
7. Serve hot, garnished with fresh cilantro leaves.

Nutritional Data:

Calories: 250 | Carbohydrates: 19g | Protein: 4g | Fats: 19g | Fiber: 5g | Sugar: 9g

Minted Pea Soup Refresh

Preparation Time: 10 minutes | Cooking Time: 20 minutes | Serves: 4

Ingredients:

- 2 tablespoons extra-virgin olive oil
- 1 medium onion, chopped
- 2 cloves garlic, minced
- 4 cups fresh or frozen peas
- 4 cups low-sodium vegetable broth
- Salt and pepper, to taste
- 1/2 cup fresh mint leaves, chopped, plus more for garnish
- 1 lemon, juiced
- 1/2 cup coconut cream

Instructions:

1. Heat the olive oil in a large pot over medium heat. Add the onions and garlic and sauté until the onions are translucent, about 5 minutes.
2. Add the peas and stir for a couple of minutes until they are well-coated with the oil and begin to soften.
3. Pour in the vegetable broth and bring the mixture to a boil. Reduce the heat to low and let it simmer for 15 minutes until the peas are tender.
4. Add the fresh mint and use an immersion blender to puree the soup until smooth. You can also carefully transfer it to a blender in batches if needed.
5. Stir in the lemon juice and season the soup with salt and pepper to taste. Let it cook for another 5 minutes to allow the flavors to meld together.
6. Ladle the soup into bowls and drizzle with coconut cream. Garnish with additional fresh mint leaves.
7. Serve warm and enjoy the refreshing flavors.

Nutritional Data:

Calories: 230 | Carbohydrates: 25g | Protein: 9g | Fats: 12g | Fiber: 8g | Sugar: 9g

Savory Mushroom & Thyme Broth

Preparation Time: 10 minutes | Cooking Time: 25 minutes | Serves: 4

Ingredients:

- 2 tablespoons olive oil
- 1 pound assorted fresh mushrooms, sliced (like shiitake, cremini, and oyster)
- 1 small onion, finely chopped
- 3 cloves garlic, minced
- 5 cups low-sodium vegetable broth
- 2 teaspoons fresh thyme leaves, plus more for garnish
- Salt and pepper to taste
- 2 tablespoons coconut aminos or low-sodium soy sauce
- Fresh parsley, chopped, for garnish

Instructions:

1. In a large pot, heat olive oil over medium heat. Add the sliced mushrooms and sauté until they are tender and release their moisture, about 7-8 minutes.
2. Add the chopped onion and minced garlic to the pot, sautéing for another 5 minutes until the onions are translucent.
3. Pour in the vegetable broth and bring the mixture to a gentle boil. Add the fresh thyme leaves and allow the mixture to simmer on low heat for 15 minutes.
4. Season the broth with salt and pepper according to your preference. Add coconut aminos or low-sodium soy sauce to enhance the flavor. Let it simmer for an additional 2 minutes.
5. Use a fine mesh strainer to strain the broth into another pot, separating the liquid from the mushroom and onions. Optionally, you can also leave the mushrooms in for a heartier soup.
6. Serve the savory mushroom and thyme broth hot, garnished with additional fresh thyme and chopped parsley.

Nutritional Data:

Calories: 110 | Carbohydrates: 8g | Protein: 4g | Fats: 7g | Fiber: 2g | Sugar: 3g

---

Tomato & Spinach Soup Essence

Preparation Time: 15 minutes | Cooking Time: 20 minutes | Serves: 4

Ingredients:

- 2 tablespoons olive oil
- 1 medium onion, chopped
- 3 cloves garlic, minced
- 1 can (28 ounces) of no-salt-added diced tomatoes
- 4 cups of low-sodium vegetable broth
- 2 cups of fresh spinach leaves, chopped
- 1 teaspoon Italian seasoning
- Salt and pepper to taste
- 1 tablespoon of fresh basil, chopped, for garnish

Instructions:

1. In a large pot, heat the olive oil over medium heat. Add the chopped onions and minced garlic, and sauté until the onions are soft and translucent, about 5 minutes.
2. Add the diced tomatoes (with their juice) to the pot, stirring well to combine with the onions and garlic.
3. Pour the low-sodium vegetable broth into the pot. Increase the heat to bring the mixture to a boil.
4. Once boiling, reduce the heat to low and stir in the Italian seasoning. Allow the soup to simmer for about 10 minutes, letting the flavors meld together.
5. Add the chopped spinach leaves to the pot, stirring to combine. Allow the soup to continue simmering until the spinach is wilted and tender, about another 5 minutes.
6. Taste the soup and add salt and pepper according to your preference. Stir well to combine.

7. Serve the tomato and spinach soup hot, garnished with a sprinkle of fresh, chopped basil on top.

Nutritional Data:

Calories: 125 | Carbohydrates: 14g | Protein: 3g | Fats: 7g | Fiber: 4g | Sugar: 8g

---

Quick Fix Veggie Pho

Preparation Time: 10 minutes | Cooking Time: 20 minutes | Serves: 4

Ingredients:

- 6 cups vegetable broth (low-sodium)
- 2 star anise
- 1 cinnamon stick
- 3 cloves garlic, minced
- 1 tablespoon ginger, grated
- 200g flat rice noodles
- 2 cups mixed fresh vegetables (like bell peppers, mushrooms, carrots), sliced
- 2 tablespoons low-sodium soy sauce
- Toppings: fresh cilantro, bean sprouts, lime wedges

Instructions:

1. In a large pot, add vegetable broth, star anise, cinnamon stick, garlic, and ginger. Bring to a boil over medium heat.
2. Once boiling, reduce the heat and let it simmer for about 15 minutes to infuse the flavors.
3. In the meantime, prepare the rice noodles according to the package instructions. Typically, they need to soak in hot water for about 5-10 minutes.
4. Using a strainer, remove the star anise and cinnamon stick from the broth and discard them.
5. Increase the heat to medium and add the sliced vegetables to the broth. Cook them for about 3-5 minutes or until they are tender but still vibrant in color.

6. Stir in the low-sodium soy sauce and adjust the seasoning if necessary.
7. Divide the cooked rice noodles into four bowls. Pour the hot veggie-infused broth over the noodles.
8. Serve immediately, topped with fresh cilantro, bean sprouts, and a squeeze of lime for added zing.

Nutritional Data:

Calories: 210 | Carbohydrates: 42g | Protein: 6g | Fats: 1g | Fiber: 3g | Sugar: 4g

Curried Lentil Soup Warmth

Preparation Time: 15 minutes | Cooking Time: 25 minutes | Serves: 4

Ingredients:

- 1 tablespoon olive oil
- 1 onion, chopped
- 3 cloves garlic, minced
- 2 carrots, peeled and diced
- 1 tablespoon curry powder
- 1 teaspoon turmeric
- 1 cup dried lentils, rinsed
- 4 cups low-sodium vegetable broth
- 1 can (14 oz) diced tomatoes; no salt added
- 2 cups spinach leaves, chopped
- Salt and pepper to taste
- 2 tablespoons fresh cilantro, chopped (for garnish)

Instructions:

1. In a large pot, heat the olive oil over medium heat. Add the chopped onion and garlic and sauté until the onions are translucent, about 5 minutes.
2. Stir in the diced carrots and cook for an additional 5 minutes, or until the carrots start to soften.
3. Sprinkle the curry powder and turmeric over the vegetables and stir well to combine. Cook for another minute to toast the spices lightly.
4. Add the rinsed lentils, vegetable broth, and diced tomatoes to the pot. Increase the heat to bring the mixture to a boil.
5. Once boiling, reduce the heat to low and let the soup simmer, covered, for about 15-20 minutes, or until the lentils are tender.
6. Remove the pot from the heat and stir in the chopped spinach. Allow the residual heat to wilt the spinach.
7. Taste and season with salt and pepper as needed. Be mindful of the sodium to align with the Galveston diet principles.
8. Serve the soup hot, garnished with fresh chopped cilantro.

Nutritional Data:

Calories: 270 | Carbohydrates: 40g | Protein: 14g | Fats: 5g | Fiber: 17g | Sugar: 8g

Spicy Black Bean Soup Burst

Preparation Time: 10 minutes | Cooking Time: 30 minutes | Serves: 4

Ingredients:

- 2 tablespoons olive oil
- 1 medium onion, chopped
- 3 cloves garlic, minced
- 1 red bell pepper, diced
- 2 cans (15 oz each) black beans, rinsed and drained
- 4 cups low-sodium vegetable broth
- 1 teaspoon cumin
- 1/2 teaspoon chili powder
- 1/2 teaspoon paprika
- Salt and pepper to taste
- 1 tablespoon lime juice
- Fresh cilantro for garnish

Instructions:

1. Heat olive oil in a large pot over medium heat. Add the chopped onion, garlic, and red bell pepper. Sauté for about 5-7 minutes, until the vegetables are softened.
2. Pour in the black beans and vegetable broth, then stir in cumin, chili powder, paprika, salt, and pepper. Adjust the seasoning according to your taste preference, keeping the Galveston diet's low sodium focus in mind.
3. Bring the soup to a boil. Once boiling, reduce the heat and let it simmer for about 20-25 minutes to allow the flavors to meld together.
4. Use an immersion blender to slightly blend the soup in the pot, leaving some chunks of beans and vegetables for texture. If you don't have an immersion blender, transfer about half of the soup to a blender, blend until smooth, and then return it to the pot.
5. Stir in the lime juice and adjust the seasoning if needed.
6. Serve the soup hot, garnished with fresh cilantro, and if desired, a dollop of yogurt or a sprinkle of cheese, adhering to the protein and healthy fats focus of the Galveston diet.

Nutritional Data:

Calories: 220 | Carbohydrates: 32g | Protein: 11g | Fats: 6g | Fiber: 12g | Sugar: 4g

Garlic & Herb Chicken Soup

Preparation Time: 15 minutes | Cooking Time: 30 minutes | Serves: 4

Ingredients:

- 2 tablespoons olive oil
- 1 pound skinless, boneless chicken breasts, cut into bite-sized pieces
- 1 large onion, chopped
- 5 cloves garlic, minced
- 4 cups low-sodium chicken broth
- 2 medium carrots, sliced
- 2 stalks celery, chopped
- 1 zucchini, chopped
- 1 tablespoon Italian seasoning
- Salt and pepper to taste
- 2 tablespoons fresh parsley, chopped
- 1 tablespoon lemon juice

Instructions:

1. In a large pot, heat the olive oil over medium heat. Add the chicken pieces and cook until they are no longer pink. Remove the chicken and set aside.
2. In the same pot, add a bit more oil if needed, then sauté the onions and garlic until they become fragrant and the onions are translucent.
3. Return the cooked chicken to the pot. Add the chicken broth, carrots, celery, and zucchini. Stir well.
4. Season the soup with Italian seasoning, salt, and pepper. Remember to moderate the salt to remain in adherence to the Galveston diet principles.

5. Bring the soup to a boil, then reduce the heat and let it simmer for about 20 minutes until the vegetables are tender.
6. Just before serving, stir in the fresh parsley and lemon juice. Adjust seasoning if necessary.
7. Serve hot and enjoy the blend of flavors, ensuring a meal rich in proteins, and low in carbs, and incorporating a mix of colorful vegetables for an antioxidant boost.

Nutritional Data:

Calories: 260 | Carbohydrates: 10g | Protein: 28g | Fats: 12g | Fiber: 3g | Sugar: 5g

---

Roasted Veggie Puree Pleasure

Preparation Time: 15 minutes | Cooking Time: 25 minutes | Serves: 4

Ingredients:

- 1 large sweet potato, peeled and chopped
- 1 red bell pepper, seeded and sliced
- 1 zucchini, sliced
- 1 yellow squash, sliced
- 1 small red onion, chopped
- 3 cloves of garlic, minced
- 2 tablespoons olive oil
- Salt and pepper to taste
- 1 teaspoon Italian seasoning
- 4 cups low-sodium vegetable broth
- 2 tablespoons fresh basil, chopped
- 1 tablespoon lemon juice

Instructions:

1. Preheat your oven to 425°F (220°C).
2. Place the sweet potato, bell pepper, zucchini, yellow squash, onion, and garlic on a large baking sheet.
3. Drizzle with olive oil, and season with salt, pepper, and Italian seasoning. Toss to coat the veggies evenly. Remember to use salt sparingly to maintain the Galveston diet's focus on reducing sodium intake.

4. Roast the veggies in the preheated oven for about 20 minutes, or until they are tender and starting to brown.
5. Remove the veggies from the oven and let them cool slightly.
6. Place the roasted veggies in a blender or food processor. Add a cup of vegetable broth and blend until smooth. If you prefer a chunkier texture, pulse the blender a few times.
7. Transfer the puree to a large pot and place it over medium heat. Stir in the remaining vegetable broth, adjusting the amount to achieve your desired soup consistency.
8. Let the soup heat up for about 5 minutes, stirring occasionally. Stir in the fresh basil and lemon juice.
9. Serve the soup hot, garnished with a few fresh basil leaves on top if desired.

Nutritional Data:

Calories: 140 | Carbohydrates: 23g | Protein: 3g | Fats: 5g | Fiber: 4g | Sugar: 9g

---

Sweet Potato Spice Soup

Preparation Time: 15 minutes | Cooking Time: 30 minutes | Serves: 4

Ingredients:

- 2 large sweet potatoes, peeled and diced
- 1 tablespoon olive oil
- 1 small onion, diced
- 3 cloves garlic, minced
- 1 teaspoon cumin
- 1/2 teaspoon cinnamon
- 1/4 teaspoon paprika
- 4 cups low-sodium chicken or vegetable broth
- 1 can (13.5 oz) coconut milk
- Salt and pepper to taste
- Fresh coriander, for garnish

Instructions:

1. Heat the olive oil in a large pot over medium heat. Add the onion and garlic and sauté until the onion is translucent, about 5 minutes.

2. Stir in the cumin, cinnamon, and paprika, cooking for another minute until the spices are fragrant.

3. Add the diced sweet potatoes to the pot and stir to coat with the spices.

4. Pour in the low-sodium broth and bring the mixture to a boil. Remember, reducing sodium is a key aspect of the Galveston diet.

5. Once boiling, reduce the heat to low, cover the pot, and let it simmer for about 20 minutes, or until the sweet potatoes are tender.

6. Use an immersion blender to puree the soup until smooth. Alternatively, you can carefully transfer the soup to a regular blender in batches and blend until smooth.

7. Return the soup to the stove and stir in the coconut milk, warming the soup over low heat. Taste and adjust the seasoning with salt and pepper, keeping in mind the Galveston diet's approach to minimal salt use.

8. Serve the soup hot, garnished with a sprinkle of fresh coriander.

Nutritional Data:

Calories: 260 | Carbohydrates: 32g | Protein: 4g | Fats: 14g | Fiber: 5g | Sugar: 10g

Rapid Rustic Minestrone

Preparation Time: 10 minutes | Cooking Time: 20 minutes | Serves: 6

Ingredients:

- 2 tablespoons olive oil
- 1 medium onion, diced
- 3 cloves garlic, minced
- 2 carrots, diced
- 2 celery stalks, diced
- 1 zucchini, diced
- 1 cup chopped spinach
- 1 can (15 oz) low-sodium chickpeas, rinsed and drained
- 1 can (14.5 oz) no-salt-added diced tomatoes
- 4 cups low-sodium vegetable broth
- 2 teaspoons Italian seasoning
- Salt and pepper to taste
- 1/2 cup whole grain or legume pasta
- Fresh basil for garnish
- Grated Parmesan cheese (optional, for serving)

Instructions:

1. Heat the olive oil in a large pot over medium heat. Add the onion and garlic and sauté until softened, about 3-4 minutes.

2. Stir in the carrots, celery, and zucchini. Sauté for another 5 minutes, or until the vegetables begin to soften.

3. Add the chickpeas, diced tomatoes (with their juice), vegetable broth, and Italian seasoning. Bring the mixture to a boil, then reduce the heat to low.

4. In another pot, cook the pasta according to package instructions but reduce the cooking time by 2 minutes so it remains slightly undercooked.

5. Add the partially cooked pasta and chopped spinach to the soup. Continue to cook for another 5 minutes, or until the pasta is cooked through and the spinach is wilted. Season with salt and pepper to taste, considering the Galveston diet's focus on reduced sodium.

6. Serve the minestrone hot, garnished with fresh basil and a sprinkle of Parmesan cheese if desired, ensuring to keep the portion moderate to maintain alignment with the Galveston diet.

Nutritional Data:

Calories: 210 | Carbohydrates: 32g | Protein: 8g | Fats: 6g | Fiber: 8g | Sugar: 7g

Thai Infusion Coconut Soup

Preparation Time: 15 minutes | Cooking Time: 25 minutes | Serves: 4

Ingredients:

- 1 tablespoon coconut oil
- 1 small onion, sliced
- 3 cloves garlic, minced
- 1 tablespoon fresh grated ginger
- 1 red bell pepper, sliced
- 1 cup sliced mushrooms
- 4 cups low-sodium vegetable broth
- 1 can (13.5 oz) full-fat coconut milk
- 2 tablespoons Thai red curry paste
- 2 tablespoons fish sauce (optional, can substitute with soy sauce for a vegetarian version)
- 1 tablespoon low-sodium soy sauce
- 1 teaspoon honey or a sugar substitute
- 2 cups cooked, peeled, and deveined shrimp or tofu cubes for a vegetarian option
- 1/4 cup fresh cilantro, chopped
- 1/4 cup fresh basil leaves, torn
- Juice of 1 lime

Instructions:

1. In a large pot, heat the coconut oil over medium heat. Add the onion, garlic, and ginger, and sauté for about 5 minutes until the onion becomes translucent.

2. Add the red bell pepper and mushrooms, and continue sautéing for an additional 5 minutes.

3. Stir in the Thai red curry paste until the vegetables are coated and the paste is fragrant.

4. Pour in the vegetable broth, coconut milk, fish or soy sauce, and soy sauce. Bring the mixture to a boil, then reduce the heat to allow it to simmer.

5. Add in the shrimp or tofu and let the soup simmer for another 10 minutes. Ensure the shrimp is cooked through and turns pink if using.

6. Remove the soup from heat, and stir in the lime juice, fresh cilantro, and basil. Adjust the seasoning if necessary, keeping in mind the Galveston diet's guidelines.

7. Serve hot, and enjoy a fragrant, flavorful soup that combines the richness of coconut milk with the aromatic Thai spices, balancing both nutrition and taste.

Nutritional Data:

Calories: 280 | Carbohydrates: 14g | Protein: 20g (with shrimp) or 12g (with tofu) | Fats: 18g | Fiber: 2g | Sugar: 6g

The Elegant Dance of Poultry Delights

Welcome back, esteemed reader, to another enlightening chapter of "The Galveston Diet for Beginners." We now spread our wings and soar into the enchanting realm of poultry recipes, where flavors, aromas, and nourishment take flight in unison. This section isn't just a compilation of recipes; it's a curated experience where the tender, savory essence of poultry is expertly intertwined with the empowering principles of the Galveston diet.

A Ballet of Flavors
Imagine the tender, succulent textures of chicken, turkey, and other poultry, meticulously marinated, seasoned, and cooked to perfection. Each recipe within these pages is a dance of flavors and textures, where poultry isn't just a source of protein but the star of a culinary ballet, each movement, each note, echoing the harmony of taste and nutrition.

The Galveston Touch
With the guiding light of the Galveston diet illuminating our path, each poultry dish is a blend of meticulously selected ingredients that honor the body's innate wisdom. It's a dance of proteins, fats, and micronutrients, choreographed to the harmonious tunes of wellness, vitality, and satisfaction.

A Flight into Wellness
Every recipe is an invitation to embark upon a flight of sensory and nutritional delight. As you peruse these pages, imagine the sizzling sounds, the alluring aromas, and the divine tastes that await. Each dish is a crafted narrative, weaving together the tender, savory notes of poultry with the vibrant, refreshing touches of herbs, spices, and accompaniments.

Your Culinary Wings Await
Dear reader, are you ready to unfurl your culinary wings and take flight into a world where every bite is an exploration, every aroma a sonnet, and every dish a masterpiece of the Galveston diet's elegance? In this chapter, we don't just cook; we compose, we create, and we celebrate. A world of poultry delights, each echoing the profound dance of taste and well-being, awaits your gracious presence.

With a heart pulsating with excitement and hands warmed by the tender embrace of culinary affection, I invite you to step into a world where poultry is not just food but a soulful journey, a delightful dance of flavors, and a heartfelt ode to the radiant health promised by the Galveston diet.

Quick Lemon-Herb Grilled Chicken

Preparation Time: 10 minutes | Cooking Time: 15 minutes | Portion Size: 4 servings

Ingredients:

- 4 boneless, skinless chicken breasts
- 2 lemons, juiced and zested
- 3 tablespoons olive oil
- 2 cloves garlic, minced
- 1 tablespoon chopped fresh rosemary
- 1 tablespoon chopped fresh thyme
- Salt and pepper to taste

Instructions:

1. In a bowl, mix the olive oil, lemon juice, lemon zest, minced garlic, chopped rosemary, and thyme to create the marinade.
2. Season the chicken breasts with salt and pepper, and then place them in a resealable plastic bag or shallow dish.
3. Pour the marinade over the chicken, ensuring each piece is well coated. Let it marinate for at least 30 minutes; for best results, leave it for a couple of hours in the refrigerator.
4. Preheat the grill to medium heat. Remove the chicken from the marinade and discard the excess marinade.
5. Grill the chicken breasts for about 6-7 minutes per side, or until they are fully cooked and have an internal temperature of 165°F (75°C).
6. Remove the chicken from the grill and let it rest for a few minutes to allow the juices to redistribute.
7. Slice and serve the lemon-herb grilled chicken on a platter or individual plates, garnished with additional fresh herbs or lemon slices if desired.

Nutritional Data:

Calories: 270 | Protein: 30g | Carbs: 4g | Fat: 15g | Fiber: 1g | Sugar: 1g

Spicy Chicken & Veggie Stir-Fry

Preparation Time: 15 minutes | Cooking Time: 20 minutes | Portion Size: 4 servings

Ingredients:

- 1 pound chicken breast, cut into bite-sized pieces
- 2 tablespoons olive oil
- 1 red bell pepper, sliced
- 1 zucchini, sliced
- 1 carrot, julienned
- 2 cloves garlic, minced
- 1 tablespoon grated ginger
- 2 tablespoons low-sodium soy sauce or tamari
- 1 tablespoon sriracha or another hot sauce (adjust to taste)
- 1 tablespoon sesame seeds
- 2 green onions, sliced
- Salt and pepper to taste

Instructions:

1. Heat 1 tablespoon of olive oil in a large skillet or wok over medium-high heat.
2. Season the chicken pieces with salt and pepper and add them to the skillet. Cook for 5-7 minutes, or until the chicken is browned and cooked through. Remove the chicken from the skillet and set it aside.
3. In the same skillet, add another tablespoon of olive oil. Stir in the minced garlic and grated ginger and sauté for about a minute until fragrant.
4. Add the sliced bell pepper, zucchini, and julienned carrot to the skillet. Stir-fry the vegetables for about 5 minutes, or until they are tender but still crisp.
5. In a small bowl, mix the soy sauce or tamari and sriracha or hot sauce. Adjust the spiciness to your liking.
6. Return the cooked chicken to the skillet with the vegetables. Pour the sauce over the top and toss everything together to combine.

7. Cook for an additional 2-3 minutes to heat the chicken through and melt the flavors.
8. Garnish the stir-fry with sesame seeds and sliced green onions before serving.
9. Serve the stir-fry warm over a bed of cauliflower rice or enjoy it as is for a low-carb, vegetable-rich meal.

Nutritional Data:

Calories: 300 | Protein: 28g | Carbs: 12g | Fat: 16g | Fiber: 3g | Sugar: 6g

---

Garlic Butter Chicken Bites

Preparation Time: 10 minutes | Cooking Time: 12 minutes | Portion Size: 4 servings

Ingredients:

- 1 pound chicken breast, cut into bite-sized pieces
- Salt and pepper to taste
- 2 tablespoons olive oil
- 4 cloves garlic, minced
- 3 tablespoons unsalted butter
- 1 teaspoon red chili flakes (optional, for added heat)
- 2 tablespoons freshly chopped parsley

Instructions:

1. Season the bite-sized chicken pieces generously with salt and pepper.
2. Heat the olive oil in a large skillet over medium heat. Add the chicken pieces and cook them until they're golden brown and cooked through, typically about 5-7 minutes. Remove the chicken from the skillet and set it aside.
3. In the same skillet, melt the butter. Add the minced garlic (and red chili flakes if desired) and sauté for about 1 minute or until the garlic becomes fragrant.
4. Return the cooked chicken bites to the skillet and toss them to coat in the garlic butter mixture. Cook for another 2-3

minutes until the chicken is heated through and absorbs the flavors.
5. Remove the skillet from the heat and sprinkle the freshly chopped parsley over the top to garnish.
6. Serve the garlic butter chicken bites as a delicious appetizer or pair them with a side of steamed vegetables or salad for a complete meal.

Nutritional Data:

Calories: 280 | Protein: 25g | Carbs: 2g | Fat: 19g | Fiber: 0g | Sugar: 0g

---

Tangy Balsamic Glazed Chicken

Preparation Time: 10 minutes | Cooking Time: 20 minutes | Portion Size: 4 servings

Ingredients:

- 4 boneless, skinless chicken breasts
- Salt and pepper to taste
- 2 tablespoons olive oil
- 4 cloves garlic, minced
- 1/2 cup balsamic vinegar
- 2 tablespoons honey
- 1 tablespoon Dijon mustard
- 1 teaspoon dried rosemary or 1 tablespoon fresh, chopped
- Optional: sliced green onions or fresh parsley for garnish

Instructions:

1. Season the chicken breasts with salt and pepper on both sides.
2. In a large skillet, heat the olive oil over medium heat. Add the chicken and cook for about 6-7 minutes on each side or until it's fully cooked and has a nice golden brown color. Remove the chicken from the skillet and set aside.
3. In the same skillet, add the minced garlic and sauté for about a minute, just until it becomes fragrant.

4. Pour in the balsamic vinegar, stirring to deglaze the pan, and pick up any flavorful bits left behind from the chicken.

5. Stir in the honey, Dijon mustard, and rosemary. Allow the sauce to simmer for about 5 minutes, or until it begins to thicken slightly.

6. Return the chicken to the skillet, spooning some of the sauce over the top of each breast. Let it cook for an additional 2-3 minutes to allow the chicken to absorb some of the flavors and the sauce to thicken further.

7. Serve the chicken hot, drizzled with the remaining balsamic glaze. Garnish with sliced green onions or fresh parsley if desired.

Nutritional Data:

Calories: 285 | Protein: 25g | Carbs: 15g | Fat: 13g | Fiber: 0g | Sugar: 13g

Savory Rosemary Chicken Skewers

Preparation Time: 15 minutes (plus marinating time) | Cooking Time: 10 minutes | Portion Size: 4 servings

Ingredients:

- 1 pound chicken breast, cut into bite-sized pieces
- 2 tablespoons olive oil
- 3 tablespoons fresh rosemary, finely chopped
- 2 cloves garlic, minced
- 1 lemon, juiced
- Salt and pepper to taste
- 8 wooden skewers, soaked in water for at least 30 minutes

Instructions:

1. In a mixing bowl, combine olive oil, chopped rosemary, minced garlic, lemon juice, salt, and pepper to make the marinade.

2. Add the chicken pieces to the bowl, tossing them well to ensure they are fully coated with the marinade. Cover and let the chicken marinate for at least 30 minutes in the refrigerator. For the best flavor, let it marinate for up to 2 hours.

3. Preheat the grill to medium-high heat. While the grill is heating, thread the marinated chicken pieces onto the soaked wooden skewers.

4. Place the chicken skewers on the grill. Cook for about 5 minutes on each side or until the chicken is fully cooked and has nice grill marks.

5. Remove the skewers from the grill and let them rest for a few minutes before serving.

6. Serve the savory rosemary chicken skewers with a side of grilled vegetables or a fresh salad for a complete, balanced meal.

Nutritional Data:

Calories: 200 | Protein: 25g | Carbs: 3g | Fat: 10g | Fiber: 1g | Sugar: 1g

Spiced Chicken & Quinoa Bowl

Preparation Time: 15 minutes | Cooking Time: 20 minutes | Portion Size: 4 servings

Ingredients:

- 1 pound chicken breast, cut into bite-sized pieces
- 1 cup quinoa, rinsed
- 2 tablespoons olive oil
- 1 teaspoon paprika
- 1 teaspoon cumin
- 1/2 teaspoon turmeric
- Salt and pepper to taste
- 2 cups mixed vegetables (like bell peppers, cherry tomatoes, and spinach)
- 1 avocado, sliced
- 1 lemon, juiced

Instructions:

1. In a small pot, cook the quinoa according to package instructions. Set aside.
2. While the quinoa is cooking, season the chicken pieces with paprika, cumin, turmeric, salt, and pepper.
3. Heat the olive oil in a large skillet over medium heat. Add the seasoned chicken and cook for 5-7 minutes until fully cooked and golden brown.
4. Remove the chicken from the skillet and set aside. In the same skillet, add the mixed vegetables and sauté for about 5 minutes until they are tender yet still vibrant.
5. In a large bowl, combine the cooked quinoa, spiced chicken, and sautéed vegetables. Toss everything together to mix well.
6. Divide the mixture into four serving bowls. Top each bowl with slices of avocado and a drizzle of fresh lemon juice for an added zesty flavor.
7. Serve immediately and enjoy the colorful, flavorful, and nutritious bowl brimming with the wholesome goodness of grains, proteins, and vegetables.

Nutritional Data:

Calories: 420 | Protein: 30g | Carbs: 35g | Fat: 18g | Fiber: 8g | Sugar: 5g

Honey-Mustard Chicken Salad

Preparation Time: 15 minutes | Cooking Time: 20 minutes | Portion Size: 4 servings

Ingredients:

- 1 pound chicken breast, grilled and sliced
- 8 cups mixed salad greens (like arugula, spinach, and romaine)
- 1 cup cherry tomatoes, halved
- 1/2 cup cucumber, sliced
- 1/4 cup red onion, thinly sliced
- 2 tablespoons olive oil
- 2 tablespoons honey
- 2 tablespoons Dijon mustard
- 1 tablespoon apple cider vinegar
- Salt and pepper to taste
- 2 tablespoons sliced almonds for garnish

Instructions:

1. In a small bowl, whisk together the honey, Dijon mustard, apple cider vinegar, salt, and pepper to make the dressing. Set aside.
2. In a large salad bowl, combine the mixed greens, cherry tomatoes, cucumber, and red onion.
3. Drizzle the olive oil over the salad and toss gently to coat the vegetables.
4. Add the grilled and sliced chicken breast on top of the salad.
5. Drizzle the honey-mustard dressing over the chicken and salad. Toss again to ensure everything is nicely coated with the dressing.
6. Divide the salad into four serving bowls.
7. Garnish each bowl with a sprinkle of sliced almonds to add a crunchy texture and extra flavor.
8. Serve immediately and enjoy this refreshing, flavorful, and nutritious salad.

Nutritional Data:

Calories: 330 | Protein: 28g | Carbs: 18g | Fat: 16g | Fiber: 4g | Sugar: 12g

Skillet Chicken with Spinach & Tomatoes

Preparation Time: 10 minutes | Cooking Time: 20 minutes | Portion Size: 4 servings

Ingredients:

- 4 chicken breasts, boneless and skinless
- 2 tablespoons olive oil
- 3 cloves garlic, minced
- 2 cups cherry tomatoes, halved
- 4 cups fresh spinach
- 1/2 cup chicken broth
- Salt and pepper to taste
- 1 tablespoon Italian seasoning
- 1/4 cup grated Parmesan cheese (optional)
- Fresh basil leaves for garnish

Instructions:

1. Season the chicken breasts with salt, pepper, and Italian seasoning on both sides.
2. In a large skillet, heat the olive oil over medium heat. Add the chicken breasts and cook for about 5-7 minutes on each side or until they are fully cooked and have a golden-brown exterior. Remove the chicken from the skillet and set aside.
3. In the same skillet, add the minced garlic and sauté for about a minute until aromatic.
4. Add the halved cherry tomatoes to the skillet and cook for another 2-3 minutes until they start to soften.
5. Pour in the chicken broth and bring the mixture to a gentle simmer.
6. Add the fresh spinach to the skillet. Cook for 2-3 minutes until the spinach wilts.
7. Return the cooked chicken breasts to the skillet, nestling them into the spinach and tomatoes. Allow everything to cook together for another 3-4 minutes.
8. If desired, sprinkle the grated Parmesan cheese over the top and allow it to melt.
9. Garnish with fresh basil leaves for an added pop of color and flavor.
10. Serve the skillet chicken with a side of cauliflower rice or enjoy it as is for a lower carb option.

Nutritional Data:

Calories: 290 | Protein: 35g | Carbs: 8g | Fat: 12g | Fiber: 2g | Sugar: 4g

Easy-Peasy Chicken Fajitas

Preparation Time: 15 minutes | Cooking Time: 15 minutes | Portion Size: 4 servings

Ingredients:

- 1 pound chicken breast, thinly sliced
- 1 red bell pepper, sliced
- 1 yellow bell pepper, sliced
- 1 onion, sliced
- 2 tablespoons olive oil
- 1 teaspoon chili powder
- 1 teaspoon cumin
- 1 teaspoon paprika
- Salt and pepper to taste
- 2 tablespoons fresh lime juice
- 2 tablespoons fresh cilantro, chopped
- Lettuce leaves for serving (optional)

Instructions:

1. In a mixing bowl, combine the sliced chicken with chili powder, cumin, paprika, salt, and pepper. Toss everything together to ensure the chicken is well-coated with the seasonings.
2. Heat one tablespoon of olive oil in a large skillet over medium heat.
3. Add the seasoned chicken to the skillet and cook for 5-7 minutes until fully cooked and slightly crispy. Remove the chicken from the skillet and set aside.
4. In the same skillet, add another tablespoon of olive oil. Add the sliced bell peppers and onions. Sauté the vegetables for about 5 minutes until they are tender and vibrant.
5. Return the cooked chicken to the skillet and mix with the sautéed vegetables. Drizzle the fresh lime juice over the top and toss everything together.
6. Remove the skillet from the heat and sprinkle the fresh chopped cilantro over the chicken fajitas for a burst of flavor.

7. Serve the chicken fajitas in lettuce leaves for a low-carb option or enjoy them as is, garnished with extra lime wedges and a dollop of guacamole if desired.

Nutritional Data:

Calories: 260 | Protein: 28g | Carbs: 10g | Fat: 12g | Fiber: 3g | Sugar: 6g

Cilantro-Lime Chicken Tacos

Preparation Time: 20 minutes | Cooking Time: 20 minutes | Portion Size: 4 servings

Ingredients:

- 1 pound chicken breast, cut into strips
- 2 tablespoons olive oil
- Juice of 2 limes
- 3 tablespoons fresh cilantro, chopped
- 1 teaspoon chili powder
- 1 teaspoon cumin
- Salt and pepper to taste
- 1 avocado, sliced
- 1 cup cherry tomatoes, halved
- 8 lettuce leaves (as taco shells)
- 1/2 cup red cabbage, shredded (optional for garnish)

Instructions:

1. In a bowl, mix the olive oil, lime juice, half of the chopped cilantro, chili powder, cumin, salt, and pepper to make a marinade.
2. Place the chicken strips in the marinade, ensuring they are well-coated. Let them marinate for at least 15 minutes. If time permits, let them marinate for an hour in the refrigerator for enhanced flavor.
3. Heat a skillet over medium heat. Cook the marinated chicken strips for 5-7 minutes on each side, or until they are fully cooked and have a golden exterior.
4. While the chicken is cooking, prepare the "taco shells" using lettuce leaves. Lay them out and ready for assembling.

5. Once the chicken is cooked, assemble the tacos. Place a few cooked chicken strips on each lettuce leaf.
6. Garnish each taco with sliced avocado, halved cherry tomatoes, and the remaining fresh cilantro. Add shredded red cabbage on top for an extra crunch and color, if desired.
7. Serve the cilantro-lime chicken tacos immediately, accompanied by extra lime wedges to drizzle over the top.

Nutritional Data:

Calories: 300 | Protein: 30g | Carbs: 12g | Fat: 16g | Fiber: 6g | Sugar: 4g

Turmeric Spiced Chicken Wraps

Preparation Time: 15 minutes | Cooking Time: 15 minutes | Portion Size: 4 servings

Ingredients:

- 1 pound of chicken breast, sliced
- 1 tablespoon olive oil
- 2 teaspoons turmeric powder
- 1 teaspoon paprika
- Salt and pepper to taste
- 4 large lettuce leaves (for wrapping)
- 1 avocado, sliced
- 1/2 cup cherry tomatoes, sliced
- 1/4 cup red onions, thinly sliced
- 2 tablespoons tahini sauce (optional for drizzling)

Instructions:

1. In a bowl, mix the sliced chicken with turmeric, paprika, salt, and pepper until it's well-coated.
2. Heat the olive oil in a skillet over medium heat. Add the chicken slices and cook for about 5-7 minutes on each side, until they're fully cooked and have a golden hue.
3. While the chicken is cooking, prepare your vegetables. Slice the avocados, cherry tomatoes, and red onions.

4. Lay out the lettuce leaves for wrapping. These will serve as your low-carb, crispy, and refreshing "tortillas."

5. Once the chicken is cooked, assemble the wraps. Place a portion of chicken on each lettuce leaf.

6. Add the sliced avocado, cherry tomatoes, and red onions over the chicken.

7. For an extra flavor kick, drizzle a bit of tahini sauce over the fillings (optional).

8. Wrap the lettuce around the fillings, securing it with a toothpick if necessary. Serve immediately and enjoy this savory, spicy, and refreshing meal.

Nutritional Data:

Calories: 280 | Protein: 27g | Carbs: 8g | Fat: 16g | Fiber: 5g | Sugar: 2g

Pan-Seared Chicken & Asparagus

Preparation Time: 10 minutes | Cooking Time: 20 minutes | Portion Size: 4 servings

Ingredients:

- 4 boneless, skinless chicken breasts
- 1 bunch of asparagus, trimmed
- 2 tablespoons of olive oil
- 1 teaspoon of garlic, minced
- Salt and pepper to taste
- Lemon zest from 1 lemon
- 2 tablespoons of fresh lemon juice
- 1 tablespoon of fresh parsley, chopped (optional for garnish)

Instructions:

1. Season the chicken breasts with salt, pepper, and lemon zest evenly on both sides.

2. In a large pan, heat 1 tablespoon of olive oil over medium heat. Add the chicken breasts and cook for about 6-7 minutes on each side or until they are cooked through and have a golden-brown color. Remove the chicken from the pan and set aside.

3. In the same pan, add another tablespoon of olive oil. Add minced garlic and sauté for about a minute until fragrant.

4. Add the asparagus to the pan. Season with salt and pepper and sauté for about 7-8 minutes, or until the asparagus is tender but still vibrant green.

5. Return the cooked chicken breasts to the pan. Drizzle fresh lemon juice over the chicken and asparagus. Toss everything to combine and heat for another 2 minutes.

6. Garnish with chopped parsley and serve immediately.

Nutritional Data:

Calories: 240 | Protein: 29g | Carbs: 6g | Fat: 11g | Fiber: 2g | Sugar: 3g

Cajun Chicken & Cauliflower Rice

Preparation Time: 15 minutes | Cooking Time: 20 minutes | Portion Size: 4 servings

Ingredients:

- 4 boneless, skinless chicken breasts, cut into bite-size pieces
- 3 cups of cauliflower rice
- 2 tablespoons of olive oil
- 2 teaspoons of Cajun seasoning
- 1 red bell pepper, sliced
- 1 green bell pepper, sliced
- 1 small red onion, sliced
- 2 cloves of garlic, minced
- Salt and pepper to taste
- 2 tablespoons of chopped fresh cilantro (optional for garnish)

Instructions:

1. In a large bowl, mix the chicken pieces with Cajun seasoning, salt, and pepper. Ensure each piece is well-coated.

2. Heat 1 tablespoon of olive oil in a large skillet over medium heat. Add the chicken pieces and cook until they're browned and

cooked through. Remove the chicken from the skillet and set aside.

3. In the same skillet, add another tablespoon of olive oil. Add the garlic and sauté for about a minute until aromatic.

4. Add the bell peppers and onion to the skillet. Sauté the vegetables for about 5-6 minutes, or until they are tender and slightly caramelized.

5. Push the vegetables to the side of the skillet and add the cauliflower rice to the center. Cook for another 5-7 minutes, or until the cauliflower rice is tender.

6. Return the cooked chicken to the skillet and mix everything. Cook for another 2-3 minutes to heat the chicken.

7. Garnish with chopped cilantro and serve immediately.

Nutritional Data:

Calories: 260 | Protein: 28g | Carbs: 12g | Fat: 11g | Fiber: 4g | Sugar: 6g

Zesty Lemon-Pepper Chicken Wings

Preparation Time: 10 minutes | Cooking Time: 30 minutes | Portion Size: 4 servings

Ingredients:

- 2 lbs of chicken wings
- 1 tablespoon of olive oil
- 2 lemons, juiced and zested
- 1 tablespoon of coarsely ground black pepper
- 1 teaspoon of sea salt
- 2 cloves of garlic, minced
- 1 tablespoon of fresh parsley, chopped (optional for garnish)
- Lemon wedges, for serving

Instructions:

1. Preheat your oven to 425°F (220°C). Line a baking sheet with parchment paper or lightly grease it.

2. In a large bowl, mix the olive oil, lemon juice, lemon zest, black pepper, sea salt, and minced garlic.

3. Toss the chicken wings in the mixture until they're well-coated. Arrange the wings in a single layer on the prepared baking sheet.

4. Bake for about 25-30 minutes, or until the wings are golden brown and crispy. Flip them halfway through cooking to ensure they're evenly cooked.

5. Remove the wings from the oven and let them rest for a couple of minutes.

6. Garnish with chopped parsley and serve with lemon wedges on the side.

Nutritional Data:

Calories: 320 | Protein: 22g | Carbs: 3g | Fat: 25g | Fiber: 1g | Sugar: 0g

Sesame Ginger Chicken Stir-Fry

Preparation Time: 15 minutes | Cooking Time: 15 minutes | Portion Size: 4 servings

Ingredients:

- 1 pound of boneless, skinless chicken breasts, cut into bite-size pieces
- 2 tablespoons of sesame oil
- 1 tablespoon of freshly grated ginger
- 3 cloves garlic, minced
- 1 red bell pepper, sliced
- 1 yellow bell pepper, sliced
- 1 cup of snap peas
- 2 green onions, sliced
- 2 tablespoons of tamari or low-sodium soy sauce
- 1 tablespoon of sesame seeds
- Fresh coriander leaves, for garnish

Instructions:

1. Heat a large pan or wok over medium heat and add sesame oil.
2. Add the chicken pieces to the pan and cook until they are nicely browned and cooked through approximately 5-7 minutes. Remove the chicken from the pan and set it aside.
3. In the same pan, add a bit more oil if necessary. Add the grated ginger and minced garlic. Sauté for about a minute until aromatic.
4. Add the sliced bell peppers and snap peas to the pan. Stir-fry the vegetables for about 5 minutes, until they are tender yet crisp.
5. Return the cooked chicken to the pan. Add tamari or low-sodium soy sauce and toss everything together.
6. Cook for another 2-3 minutes, allowing the chicken to absorb the flavors.
7. Remove from heat and sprinkle with sliced green onions and sesame seeds.
8. Serve hot, garnished with fresh coriander leaves.

Nutritional Data:

Calories: 250 | Protein: 27g | Carbs: 10g | Fat: 11g | Fiber: 3g | Sugar: 5g

Herbed Chicken & Zoodle Soup

Preparation Time: 10 minutes | Cooking Time: 20 minutes | Portion Size: 4 servings

Ingredients:

- 2 tablespoons of olive oil
- 1 pound of chicken breast, diced
- Salt and pepper, to taste
- 1 onion, chopped
- 2 cloves of garlic, minced
- 4 cups of chicken broth
- 2 medium zucchinis, spiralized into noodles
- 1 teaspoon of dried thyme
- 1 teaspoon of dried rosemary
- 2 cups of baby spinach leaves
- Fresh parsley, for garnish
- Lemon slices, for serving

Instructions:

1. In a large pot, heat the olive oil over medium heat. Season the diced chicken with salt and pepper, then add it to the pot. Cook until the chicken is browned and cooked through.
2. Remove the cooked chicken from the pot and set aside. In the same pot, add the chopped onion and minced garlic. Sauté until the onion becomes translucent.
3. Add the dried thyme and rosemary to the pot, stirring to combine with the onions and garlic.
4. Pour in the chicken broth and bring the mixture to a simmer. Allow it to cook for about 10 minutes to let the flavors meld.
5. Return the cooked chicken to the pot and add the spiralized zucchini noodles (zoodles). Let the soup cook for another 5 minutes, or until the zoodles are tender.
6. Just before serving, stir in the baby spinach leaves and allow them to wilt in the hot soup.
7. Serve the soup hot, garnished with fresh parsley and a slice of lemon on the side.

Nutritional Data:

Calories: 270 | Protein: 29g | Carbs: 10g | Fat: 12g | Fiber: 2g | Sugar: 5g

Buffalo Chicken Lettuce Wraps

Preparation Time: 15 minutes | Cooking Time: 15 minutes | Portion Size: 4 servings

Ingredients:

- 1 lb boneless, skinless chicken breasts, diced
- 1 tablespoon olive oil
- Salt and pepper, to taste
- 1/2 cup buffalo sauce
- 1 teaspoon honey
- 1 teaspoon apple cider vinegar
- 8 large lettuce leaves (such as Bibb, Romaine, or Iceberg)
- 1/2 cup sliced celery
- 1/4 cup chopped green onions
- 1/4 cup blue cheese crumbles (optional)

Instructions:

1. In a skillet, heat the olive oil over medium heat. Season the diced chicken with salt and pepper and cook until browned and cooked through, about 5-7 minutes. Remove from heat.
2. In a bowl, mix the buffalo sauce, honey, and apple cider vinegar. Toss the cooked chicken in this sauce until well-coated.
3. Arrange the lettuce leaves on plates. Spoon the buffalo chicken mixture onto each leaf.
4. Garnish each wrap with sliced celery, green onions, and optional blue cheese crumbles for added flavor.
5. Serve immediately and enjoy the zesty, spicy flavors paired with the crisp, refreshing lettuce wraps.

Nutritional Data:

Calories: 210 | Protein: 25g | Carbs: 6g | Fat: 9g | Fiber: 2g | Sugar: 4

Smoky Paprika Chicken Skillet

Preparation Time: 10 minutes | Cooking Time: 20 minutes | Portion Size: 4 servings

Ingredients:

- 4 boneless, skinless chicken breasts
- 2 tablespoons olive oil
- 2 teaspoons smoked paprika
- 1 teaspoon garlic powder
- Salt and pepper, to taste
- 1 cup cherry tomatoes, halved
- 1 bell pepper, sliced
- 1 red onion, sliced
- 2 cloves garlic, minced
- Fresh parsley, for garnish

Instructions:

1. Season the chicken breasts with smoked paprika, garlic powder, salt, and pepper, ensuring they are well-coated.
2. In a large skillet, heat the olive oil over medium heat. Add the chicken breasts and cook for about 5-7 minutes on each side, or until they are fully cooked and have a nice, golden-brown sear.
3. Remove the chicken from the skillet and set it aside. In the same skillet, add the garlic, bell peppers, and onions. Sauté until they become soft and fragrant.
4. Add the cherry tomatoes to the skillet and cook for an additional 2-3 minutes. Adjust the seasoning with salt and pepper if necessary.
5. Return the cooked chicken to the skillet, nestling the pieces in among the vegetables. Allow everything to heat together for a few minutes.
6. Garnish with a sprinkle of fresh parsley before serving. Enjoy your meal hot, savoring the smoky and vibrant flavors.

Nutritional Data:

Calories: 280 | Protein: 30g | Carbs: 10g | Fat: 12g | Fiber: 3g | Sugar: 5g

One-Pan Pesto Chicken Sauté

Preparation Time: 10 minutes | Cooking Time: 15 minutes | Portion Size: 4 servings

Ingredients:

- 4 boneless, skinless chicken breasts, cut into strips
- 2 tablespoons olive oil
- Salt and pepper, to taste
- 2 cloves garlic, minced
- 1 cup cherry tomatoes, halved
- 1/4 cup homemade or store-bought pesto
- 2 cups spinach leaves
- 1 tablespoon pine nuts, for garnish
- Grated Parmesan cheese, for garnish (optional)

Instructions:

1. Season the chicken strips with salt and pepper. Heat the olive oil in a large pan over medium heat. Add the chicken and cook until it is browned and cooked through. Remove the chicken and set it aside.
2. In the same pan, add the minced garlic and sauté for about a minute, until it is fragrant but not browned.
3. Add the halved cherry tomatoes to the pan. Cook them for a couple of minutes until they are soft but still retain their shape.
4. Return the cooked chicken to the pan. Add the pesto and stir well to coat the chicken and tomatoes.
5. Add the spinach leaves to the pan. Stir until the spinach is wilted and everything is well mixed.
6. Serve the chicken and vegetable mix on plates. Garnish with a sprinkle of pine nuts and a little grated Parmesan cheese if desired.

Nutritional Data:

Calories: 320 | Protein: 28g | Carbs: 6g | Fat: 20g | Fiber: 2g | Sugar: 3g

Grilled Chicken & Rainbow Veggie Platter

Preparation Time: 15 minutes | Cooking Time: 20 minutes | Portion Size: 4 servings

Ingredients:

- 4 chicken breasts, boneless and skinless
- 1 zucchini, sliced
- 1 yellow squash, sliced
- 1 red bell pepper, sliced
- 1 orange bell pepper, sliced
- 1 red onion, sliced
- 2 tablespoons olive oil
- Salt and pepper, to taste
- 1 lemon, juiced
- 2 tablespoons fresh herbs (such as parsley, cilantro, or basil), chopped

Instructions:

1. Preheat the grill to medium heat.
2. Drizzle the olive oil over the chicken breasts and vegetables. Season them generously with salt and pepper, then toss to coat.
3. Place the chicken on the grill and cook for 6-7 minutes per side, until it's cooked through and has nice grill marks.
4. While the chicken is cooking, arrange the vegetables in a grilling basket or directly on the grill, cooking them until they are tender and slightly charred.
5. Remove the chicken and vegetables from the grill. Allow the chicken to rest for a few minutes.
6. Arrange the grilled chicken and vegetables beautifully on a platter. Drizzle lemon juice over the top and sprinkle with fresh herbs for an added burst of flavor.
7. Serve immediately, enjoying the delightful mix of the grilled flavors and fresh, vibrant colors.

Nutritional Data:

Calories: 310 | Protein: 35g | Carbs: 12g | Fat: 14g | Fiber: 3g | Sugar: 7g

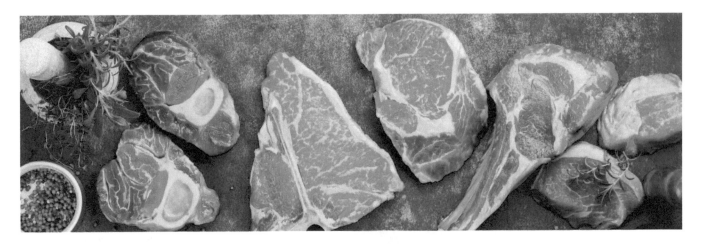

The Symphony of Succulent Meats

A hearty welcome, esteemed reader, as we venture deeper into the majestic pages of "The Galveston Diet for Beginners." We now embark upon a soul-stirring sojourn into the savory universe of meat recipes, a world where each bite is a harmonious symphony of flavors, textures, and nutrients, all serenading in unison to the melodious tunes of holistic well-being.

In this chapter, I am your culinary curator, weaving together the artistry of gourmet delights with the solid foundations of the Galveston diet. Together, we will explore a world where meat is not just a source of sustenance but a gateway to an immersive experience of sensory pleasure and nutritional abundance.

An Ode to Savoriness

In the world of meat, every morsel is an ode to savoriness, where beef, lamb, pork, and more are not merely ingredients but the keystones of delectable masterpieces. Envision the tender cuts, marinated to perfection, gracing your palate with an explosion of flavors, each bite echoing the meticulous craft of culinary artistry.

Infused with the Galveston Essence

Each recipe is infused with the enlightening essence of the Galveston diet, a beacon of wisdom guiding us through the selection of every herb, spice, and accompaniment. This is a realm where the rich, hearty textures of meat are adorned with vibrant, aromatic touches that not only tantalize the senses but also nourish the body, aligning with the soul of wellness and vitality.

A Culinary Ballet of Nutritional Harmony

Dear reader, anticipate the dance of ingredients that showcase meat in all its glory while ensuring alignment with the nutritional harmony of the Galveston diet. Each recipe is a crafted ballet where proteins, fats, and a rainbow of nutrients perform a mesmerizing dance, offering you not just a meal, but a culinary spectacle, a nutritional concerto.

The Feast Awaits

Are you prepared, dear friend, to embark on a delectable journey where meat is the majestic symphony, each note, each flavor, a heartfelt sonnet of taste and nutrition? In this chapter, the plate is not just a vessel for food but a canvas of culinary art, each recipe a painting of flavors, each bite a journey into the heart of the Galveston diet's promise.

Savory Beef & Vegetable Stir-Fry

Preparation Time: 15 minutes | Cooking Time: 15 minutes | Portion Size: 4 servings

Ingredients:

For the Stir-Fry:

- 1 pound lean beef (sirloin or flank steak), thinly sliced
- 2 tablespoons olive oil
- 1 onion, thinly sliced
- 2 bell peppers (red and green), thinly sliced
- 1 cup broccoli florets
- 1 cup snap peas, trimmed
- 3 cloves garlic, minced
- 1-inch piece of fresh ginger, minced
- 2 tablespoons low-sodium soy sauce
- 1 tablespoon rice vinegar
- 1 tablespoon honey or a sugar substitute (optional)
- 1 teaspoon cornstarch (optional, for thickening)
- Salt and pepper to taste
- Sesame seeds (optional, for garnish)
- Cooked cauliflower rice (for serving)

Instructions:

1. In a small bowl, combine the low-sodium soy sauce, rice vinegar, honey (if using), and cornstarch (if using). Set this sauce aside.
2. Heat 1 tablespoon of olive oil in a large skillet or wok over medium-high heat. Add the thinly sliced beef and stir-fry until it's browned and cooked through. Remove the beef from the skillet and set it aside.
3. In the same skillet, add the remaining tablespoon of olive oil. Add the minced garlic and ginger, and sauté for about 30 seconds until fragrant.
4. Add the sliced onion, bell peppers, broccoli florets, and snap peas to the skillet. Stir-fry for 3-4 minutes until the vegetables are tender-crisp.
5. Return the cooked beef to the skillet and pour the prepared sauce over the meat and vegetables. Toss everything together and cook for an additional 2-3 minutes until the sauce thickens and coats the ingredients evenly.
6. Season the stir-fry with salt and pepper to taste.
7. Serve the Savory Beef & Vegetable Stir-Fry over cooked cauliflower rice. If desired, garnish with sesame seeds.

Nutritional Data:

Calories: 250 | Carbohydrates: 14g | Protein: 25g | Fats: 11g | Fiber: 4g | Sugar: 7g

Quick Herb-Crusted Pork Chops

Preparation Time: 10 minutes | Cooking Time: 20 minutes | Portion Size: 4 servings

Ingredients:

For the Herb-Crusted Pork Chops:

- 4 boneless pork chops
- 2 tablespoons olive oil
- 1/2 cup whole wheat breadcrumbs
- 2 tablespoons fresh parsley, chopped
- 1 tablespoon fresh thyme leaves, chopped
- 1 teaspoon garlic powder
- 1/2 teaspoon paprika
- Salt and pepper to taste

For the Lemon Herb Sauce:

- 1/4 cup low-sodium chicken broth
- Juice of 1 lemon
- Zest of 1 lemon
- 1 tablespoon fresh basil, chopped
- 1 tablespoon fresh chives, chopped
- Salt and pepper to taste

Instructions:

1. Preheat your oven to 375°F (190°C).
2. In a mixing bowl, combine the breadcrumbs, fresh parsley, fresh thyme, garlic powder, paprika, salt, and pepper. Mix well to create the herb crust mixture.
3. Pat the pork chops dry with paper towels to remove any excess moisture.
4. Brush both sides of each pork chop with olive oil.
5. Press each pork chop firmly into the herb crust mixture, ensuring that both sides are well-coated.
6. Heat an ovenproof skillet over medium-high heat. Once hot, add the pork chops and sear for 2-3 minutes on each side until they develop a golden crust.
7. Transfer the skillet to the preheated oven and bake for 10-12 minutes or until the pork chops reach an internal temperature of 145°F (63°C).
8. While the pork chops are baking, prepare the Lemon Herb Sauce. In a small saucepan, combine the low-sodium chicken broth, lemon juice, lemon zest, fresh basil, and fresh chives. Simmer over low heat for about 5 minutes, allowing the flavors to meld. Season with salt and pepper to taste.
9. Once the pork chops are done, remove them from the oven and let them rest for a few minutes.
10. Serve the herb-crusted pork chops drizzled with the Lemon Herb Sauce.

Nutritional Data:

Nutritional Data (per serving): Calories: 280 | Carbohydrates: 12g | Protein: 30g | Fats: 12g | Fiber: 2g | Sugar: 1g

Garlic Butter Steak Bites

Preparation Time: 10 minutes | Cooking Time: 10 minutes | Portion Size: 4 servings

Ingredients:

- 1 pound sirloin steak, cut into bite-sized pieces
- 2 tablespoons olive oil
- 4 cloves garlic, minced
- 2 tablespoons unsalted butter
- 1 teaspoon fresh rosemary, minced
- 1 teaspoon fresh thyme, minced
- Salt and pepper to taste
- Fresh parsley, chopped (for garnish)

Instructions:

1. Season the bite-sized pieces of sirloin steak with salt and pepper to taste.
2. In a large skillet, heat the olive oil over medium-high heat.
3. Add the minced garlic and cook for about 1 minute until fragrant.
4. Add the seasoned steak pieces to the skillet and sear them for about 2-3 minutes on each side, or until they reach your desired level of doneness. Remove the steak from the skillet and set it aside.

5. In the same skillet, reduce the heat to low, and add the unsalted butter, minced rosemary, and minced thyme. Cook for about 1-2 minutes until the herbs are fragrant and the butter is melted.
6. Return the cooked steak bites to the skillet, tossing them in the garlic herb butter to coat evenly. Cook for an additional 1-2 minutes to reheat the steak and allow it to absorb the flavors.
7. Remove the skillet from heat.
8. Garnish the Garlic Butter Steak Bites with fresh parsley.

Nutritional Data:

Nutritional Data (per serving): Calories: 250 | Carbohydrates: 0g | Protein: 25g | Fats: 16g | Fiber: 0g | Sugar: 0g

Rosemary Infused Lamb Chops

Preparation Time: 10 minutes | Cooking Time: 15 minutes | Portion Size: 4 servings

Ingredients:

- 8 lamb chops
- 2 tablespoons olive oil
- 4 cloves garlic, minced
- 2 sprigs fresh rosemary
- Salt and pepper to taste
- Lemon wedges (for garnish)

Instructions:

1. Preheat your grill or grill pan to medium-high heat.
2. Season the lamb chops generously with salt and pepper.
3. In a small saucepan, heat the olive oil over low heat. Add the minced garlic and cook for about 1-2 minutes until it becomes fragrant. Remove the garlic-infused oil from the heat.
4. Brush both sides of each lamb chop with the garlic-infused olive oil.

5. Place the lamb chops and fresh rosemary sprigs on the preheated grill. Grill for about 3-4 minutes per side for medium-rare, adjusting the cooking time to your desired level of doneness.
6. Remove the lamb chops from the grill and let them rest for a few minutes.
7. Serve the Rosemary Infused Lamb Chops with lemon wedges for garnish.

Nutritional Data:

Nutritional Data (per serving): Calories: 300 | Carbohydrates: 0g | Protein: 25g | Fats: 22g | Fiber: 0g | Sugar: 0g

Tender Beef & Broccoli Bowl

Preparation Time: 15 minutes | Cooking Time: 15 minutes | Portion Size: 4 servings

Ingredients:

For the Beef Marinade:

- 1 pound lean beef (such as sirloin or flank steak), thinly sliced
- 2 tablespoons low-sodium soy sauce
- 1 tablespoon rice vinegar
- 1 tablespoon honey or a sugar substitute (optional)
- 1 teaspoon cornstarch (optional, for thickening)
- 2 cloves garlic, minced
- 1-inch piece of fresh ginger, minced
- Salt and pepper to taste

For the Broccoli Stir-Fry:

- 2 cups broccoli florets
- 1/4 cup low-sodium chicken or vegetable broth
- 2 tablespoons olive oil
- 2 cloves garlic, minced
- Salt and pepper to taste

For Serving:

- Cooked brown rice or cauliflower rice

Instructions:

1. In a bowl, combine the low-sodium soy sauce, rice vinegar, honey (if using), cornstarch (if using), minced garlic, minced ginger, salt, and pepper to create the beef marinade.
2. Place the thinly sliced beef in a zip-top bag or a shallow dish and pour the marinade over it. Seal the bag or cover the dish, then refrigerate for at least 15 minutes (or up to 2 hours) to marinate the beef.
3. In a large skillet or wok, heat 1 tablespoon of olive oil over medium-high heat. Add the minced garlic and cook for about 30 seconds until fragrant.
4. Add the broccoli florets to the skillet and stir-fry for 2-3 minutes.
5. Pour in the low-sodium chicken or vegetable broth, cover the skillet, and steam the broccoli for an additional 3-4 minutes until it becomes tender-crisp. Remove the broccoli from the skillet and set it aside.
6. In the same skillet, add the remaining tablespoon of olive oil.
7. Remove the marinated beef from the bag or dish, allowing any excess marinade to drip off. Add the beef to the skillet and stir-fry for about 2-3 minutes until it's browned and cooked to your desired level of doneness.
8. Return the cooked broccoli to the skillet, tossing it with the beef for an additional minute to combine flavors.
9. Serve the Tender Beef & Broccoli over cooked brown rice or cauliflower rice.

Nutritional Data:

Nutritional Data (per serving): Calories: 280 | Carbohydrates: 15g | Protein: 25g | Fats: 12g | Fiber: 3g | Sugar: 5g

Paprika Spiced Pork Tenderloin

Preparation Time: 10 minutes | Cooking Time: 25 minutes | Portion Size: 4 servings

Ingredients:

For the Paprika Spice Rub:

- 1 tablespoon smoked paprika
- 1 teaspoon garlic powder
- 1 teaspoon onion powder
- 1/2 teaspoon dried thyme
- 1/2 teaspoon dried oregano
- Salt and pepper to taste

For the Pork Tenderloin:

- 1 pound pork tenderloin
- 1 tablespoon olive oil
- 2 cloves garlic, minced
- 1 teaspoon Dijon mustard
- 1 teaspoon honey or a sugar substitute (optional)
- 1 tablespoon fresh parsley, chopped (for garnish)

Instructions:

1. Preheat your oven to 375°F (190°C).
2. In a small bowl, combine the smoked paprika, garlic powder, onion powder, dried thyme, dried oregano, salt, and pepper to create the paprika spice rub.
3. Pat the pork tenderloin dry with paper towels. Rub the spice mixture evenly over the pork.
4. Heat the olive oil in an ovenproof skillet over medium-high heat. Add the minced garlic and sauté for about 30 seconds until fragrant.
5. Add the pork tenderloin to the skillet and sear it on all sides until it develops a golden crust.
6. In a small bowl, mix the Dijon mustard and honey (if using). Brush this mixture over the seared pork.
7. Transfer the skillet with the pork to the preheated oven and roast for approximately 20-25 minutes, or until the pork reaches an internal temperature of 145°F (63°C).
8. Remove the pork from the oven and let it rest for a few minutes before slicing.

9. Garnish the Paprika Spiced Pork Tenderloin with fresh parsley before serving.

Nutritional Data:

Nutritional Data (per serving): Calories: 250 | Carbohydrates: 2g | Protein: 25g | Fats: 15g | Fiber: 1g | Sugar: 1g

---

Grilled Lamb with Mint Pesto

Preparation Time: 15 minutes | Cooking Time: 15 minutes | Portion Size: 4 servings

Ingredients:

For the Grilled Lamb:

- 1,5 pounds boneless lamb loin or leg of lamb, cut into 1-inch thick slices
- 2 tablespoons olive oil
- 2 cloves garlic, minced
- 1 teaspoon dried rosemary
- 1 teaspoon dried thyme
- Salt and pepper to taste

For the Mint Pesto:

- 1 cup fresh mint leaves, packed
- 1/4 cup fresh basil leaves, packed
- 1/4 cup unsalted almonds
- 2 cloves garlic, minced
- 1/4 cup extra-virgin olive oil
- Juice of 1 lemon
- Salt and pepper to taste

Instructions:

1. Preheat your grill to medium-high heat.
2. In a bowl, combine the olive oil, minced garlic, dried rosemary, dried thyme, salt, and pepper to create a marinade for the lamb.
3. Brush both sides of the lamb slices with the marinade.
4. Place the lamb on the preheated grill and cook for approximately 4-5 minutes per side for medium-rare, adjusting the cooking time to your desired level of doneness.

5. While the lamb is grilling, prepare the Mint Pesto. In a food processor, combine the fresh mint leaves, fresh basil leaves, unsalted almonds, minced garlic, extra-virgin olive oil, lemon juice, salt, and pepper. Pulse until you achieve a pesto-like consistency. Adjust the seasoning to your taste.
6. Once the lamb is done, remove it from the grill and let it rest for a few minutes.
7. Serve the Grilled Lamb with a generous dollop of Mint Pesto.

Nutritional Data (per serving):

Calories: 300 | Carbohydrates: 3g | Protein: 28g | Fats: 20g | Fiber: 2g | Sugar: 1g

---

Spiced Lamb Skewers Delight

Preparation Time: 20 minutes | Cooking Time: 10 minutes | Portion Size: 4 servings

Ingredients:

For the Lamb Marinade:

- 1 pound lean lamb cubes
- 2 cloves garlic, minced
- 1 tablespoon ground cumin
- 1 teaspoon ground coriander
- 1 teaspoon paprika
- 1/2 teaspoon ground cinnamon
- 2 tablespoons olive oil
- **Salt and pepper to taste**

For the Yogurt Sauce:

- 1 cup plain Greek yogurt
- 1/2 cucumber, finely grated and drained
- 2 tablespoons fresh mint leaves, chopped
- 1 tablespoon lemon juice
- Salt and pepper to taste

For Serving:

- Whole wheat pita bread or cauliflower flatbread
- Mixed greens and cherry tomatoes (optional, for garnish)

Instructions:

1. In a bowl, combine the minced garlic, ground cumin, ground coriander, paprika, ground cinnamon, olive oil, salt, and pepper to create the lamb marinade.
2. Thread the lean lamb cubes onto skewers. Place the skewers in a shallow dish and brush them with the marinade. Let them marinate for at least 15 minutes or refrigerate for up to 2 hours for more intense flavor.
3. While the lamb is marinating, prepare the yogurt sauce. In a separate bowl, mix the plain Greek yogurt, grated cucumber, chopped mint leaves, lemon juice, salt, and pepper. Refrigerate until serving.
4. Preheat a grill or grill pan to medium-high heat. Grill the lamb skewers for about 3-4 minutes per side or until they reach your desired level of doneness.
5. Warm the whole wheat pita bread or cauliflower flatbread on the grill for about 1 minute per side.
6. Serve the Spiced Lamb Skewers with the warm bread and a generous dollop of the yogurt sauce. Garnish with mixed greens and cherry tomatoes if desired.

Nutritional Data:

Nutritional Data (per serving): Calories: 300 | Carbohydrates: 14g | Protein: 28g | Fats: 15g | Fiber: 3g | Sugar: 4g.

Seared Steak & Asparagus Bundles

Preparation Time: 15 minutes | Cooking Time: 20 minutes | Portion Size: 4 servings

Ingredients:

For the Steak & Asparagus Bundles:

- 4 beef sirloin or filet mignon steaks
- 1 pound fresh asparagus spears, ends trimmed
- 2 tablespoons olive oil
- 2 cloves garlic, minced
- Salt and pepper to taste

For the Lemon-Herb Butter:

- 4 tablespoons unsalted butter, softened
- Zest of 1 lemon
- 1 tablespoon fresh thyme leaves, chopped
- Salt and pepper to taste

Instructions:

1. Preheat your oven to 400°F (200°C).
2. Season the beef steaks with salt and pepper.
3. Divide the asparagus into 4 equal portions, then wrap each portion with a steak, securing it with kitchen twine.
4. In a large ovenproof skillet, heat the olive oil over medium-high heat. Add the minced garlic and cook for about 30 seconds until fragrant.
5. Place the steak and asparagus bundles in the skillet and sear them for 2-3 minutes on

each side until the steaks develop a golden crust.

6. Transfer the skillet to the preheated oven and roast for approximately 10-12 minutes for medium-rare, adjusting the cooking time based on your preferred doneness.

7. While the steak bundles are roasting, prepare the Lemon-Herb Butter. In a small bowl, combine the softened unsalted butter, lemon zest, chopped fresh thyme leaves, salt, and pepper.

8. Once the steak bundles are done, remove them from the oven and let them rest for a few minutes.

9. Serve the Seared Steak & Asparagus Bundles with a dollop of Lemon-Herb Butter on top.

Nutritional Data (per serving):

Calories: 350 | Carbohydrates: 4g | Protein: 30g | Fats: 24g | Fiber: 2g | Sugar: 1g

Honey Glazed Pork Medallions

Preparation Time: 10 minutes | Cooking Time: 20 minutes | Portion Size: 4 servings

Ingredients:

For the Pork Medallions:

- 1 pound pork tenderloin, cut into 1-inch thick medallions
- 2 tablespoons olive oil
- Salt and pepper to taste

For the Honey Glaze:

- 2 tablespoons honey
- 1 tablespoon Dijon mustard
- 2 cloves garlic, minced
- 1 teaspoon fresh thyme leaves
- Zest of 1 lemon
- Juice of 1/2 lemon

Instructions:

1. Season the pork medallions with salt and pepper.

2. In a small bowl, whisk together the honey, Dijon mustard, minced garlic, fresh thyme leaves, lemon zest, and lemon juice to create the honey glaze.

3. Heat the olive oil in a large skillet over medium-high heat.

4. Add the pork medallions to the skillet and sear them for about 2-3 minutes on each side until they develop a golden-brown crust.

5. Pour the honey glaze over the seared pork medallions in the skillet.

6. Reduce the heat to low, cover the skillet, and simmer for an additional 10-12 minutes, or until the pork reaches an internal temperature of 145°F (63°C).

7. Remove the skillet from heat and let the pork rest for a few minutes.

8. Serve the Honey Glazed Pork Medallions with a drizzle of the remaining glaze.

Nutritional Data (per serving):

Calories: 240 | Carbohydrates: 11g | Protein: 25g | Fats: 10g | Fiber: 0g | Sugar: 9g

Lemon & Herb Roasted Lamb

Preparation Time: 15 minutes | Cooking Time: 1 hour | Portion Size: 4 servings

Ingredients:

For the Roasted Lamb:

- 1 bone-in leg of lamb (about 4-5 pounds)
- 4 cloves garlic, minced
- Zest of 2 lemons
- Juice of 2 lemons
- 2 tablespoons fresh rosemary, minced
- 2 tablespoons fresh thyme, minced
- 2 tablespoons olive oil
- Salt and pepper to taste

For Garnish:

- Fresh mint leaves, chopped

Instructions:

1. Preheat your oven to 350°F (175°C).

2. In a bowl, combine the minced garlic, lemon zest, lemon juice, minced fresh rosemary,

minced fresh thyme, olive oil, salt, and pepper to create a marinade.

3. Place the bone-in leg of lamb in a roasting pan.
4. Rub the lamb with the prepared marinade, ensuring it's evenly coated.
5. Cover the roasting pan with foil.
6. Roast the lamb in the preheated oven for approximately 45 minutes.
7. Remove the foil and continue roasting for an additional 15-20 minutes or until the lamb reaches your desired level of doneness (145°F or 63°C for medium-rare).
8. Once done, remove the lamb from the oven and let it rest for about 10 minutes before carving.
9. Slice the Lemon & Herb Roasted Lamb and garnish with fresh mint leaves.

Nutritional Data (per serving):

Calories: 350 | Carbohydrates: 2g | Protein: 40g | Fats: 19g | Fiber: 1g | Sugar: 0g

Chili Lime Beef Fajita Bowl

Preparation Time: 15 minutes | Cooking Time: 20 minutes | Portion Size: 4 servings

Ingredients:

For the Chili Lime Beef:

- 1 pound lean beef (such as flank steak or sirloin), thinly sliced
- 2 tablespoons olive oil
- 2 cloves garlic, minced
- Zest of 1 lime
- Juice of 2 limes
- 1 teaspoon chili powder
- 1 teaspoon ground cumin
- Salt and pepper to taste

For the Fajita Bowl:

- 2 bell peppers, thinly sliced (a mix of colors)
- 1 red onion, thinly sliced
- 1 tablespoon olive oil
- 1 cup cooked brown rice or cauliflower rice

- Fresh cilantro leaves, chopped (for garnish)

Instructions:

1. In a bowl, combine the olive oil, minced garlic, lime zest, lime juice, chili powder, ground cumin, salt, and pepper to create a marinade for the beef.
2. Place the thinly sliced beef in a zip-top bag or a shallow dish, and pour the marinade over it. Seal the bag or cover the dish, then refrigerate for at least 15 minutes (or up to 2 hours) to marinate the beef.
3. In a large skillet, heat 1 tablespoon of olive oil over medium-high heat.
4. Add the sliced bell peppers and red onion to the skillet. Sauté for about 5-7 minutes until they become tender-crisp. Remove them from the skillet and set them aside.
5. In the same skillet, add the marinated beef and sear for about 2-3 minutes per side until it's browned and cooked to your desired level of doneness.
6. To assemble the Fajita Bowl, divide the cooked brown rice or cauliflower rice among four bowls.
7. Top the rice with the sautéed bell peppers, red onions, and chili lime beef.
8. Garnish the Chili Lime Beef Fajita Bowl with fresh cilantro leaves.

Nutritional Data (per serving):

Calories: 300 | Carbohydrates: 20g | Protein: 25g | Fats: 12g | Fiber: 4g | Sugar: 4g

Mustard Glazed Grilled Pork

Preparation Time: 10 minutes | Cooking Time: 15 minutes | Portion Size: 4 servings

Ingredients:

For the Mustard Glaze:

- 1/4 cup Dijon mustard
- 2 tablespoons honey or a sugar substitute (optional)

- 2 cloves garlic, minced
- 1 tablespoon fresh rosemary, minced
- 1 tablespoon fresh thyme, minced
- Salt and pepper to taste

For the Grilled Pork:

- 4 boneless pork chops
- 2 tablespoons olive oil
- Salt and pepper to taste

Instructions:

1. Preheat your grill to medium-high heat.
2. In a small bowl, whisk together the Dijon mustard, honey (if using), minced garlic, minced fresh rosemary, minced fresh thyme, salt, and pepper to create the mustard glaze.
3. Season the boneless pork chops with salt and pepper.
4. Brush both sides of each pork chop with olive oil.
5. Place the pork chops on the preheated grill and cook for approximately 4-5 minutes per side, or until they reach your desired level of doneness.
6. During the last few minutes of grilling, brush the Mustard Glaze onto each side of the pork chops, allowing it to caramelize.
7. Remove the grilled pork from the heat and let it rest for a few minutes before serving.

Nutritional Data (per serving):

Calories: 250 | Carbohydrates: 8g | Protein: 25g | Fats: 12g | Fiber: 1g | Sugar: 6g

Sizzling Beef & Bell Pepper Taco

Preparation Time: 15 minutes | Cooking Time: 15 minutes | Portion Size: 4 servings

Ingredients:

For the Beef Filling:

- 1 pound lean ground beef
- 1 tablespoon olive oil
- 1 small onion, finely chopped

- 2 cloves garlic, minced
- 1 teaspoon chili powder
- 1 teaspoon ground cumin
- Salt and pepper to taste

For the Bell Pepper Topping:

- 2 bell peppers, thinly sliced (a mix of colors)
- 1 tablespoon olive oil
- Salt and pepper to taste

For Assembly:

- 8 small whole wheat or corn tortillas
- Greek yogurt or sour cream (optional, for serving)
- Fresh cilantro leaves, chopped (for garnish)

Instructions:

1. In a large skillet, heat the olive oil over medium-high heat.
2. Add the chopped onion and minced garlic to the skillet. Sauté for about 2-3 minutes until the onion becomes translucent and fragrant.

3. Add the lean ground beef to the skillet and cook, breaking it apart with a spatula, until it's browned and cooked through. Drain any excess fat if necessary.

4. Season the beef with chili powder, ground cumin, salt, and pepper. Stir well to combine. Cook for an additional 2-3 minutes to meld the flavors. Remove the beef mixture from the skillet and set it aside.

5. In the same skillet, heat another tablespoon of olive oil over medium-high heat.

6. Add the thinly sliced bell peppers and sauté for about 3-4 minutes until they become tender-crisp. Season with salt and pepper. Remove the bell peppers from the skillet and set them aside.

7. Warm the tortillas according to package instructions.

8. To assemble the Sizzling Beef & Bell Pepper Tacos, spoon a portion of the seasoned beef mixture onto each tortilla. Top with the sautéed bell peppers.

9. Garnish with chopped fresh cilantro leaves and, if desired, a dollop of Greek yogurt or sour cream.

Nutritional Data (per serving, without optional toppings):

Calories: 300 | Carbohydrates: 25g | Protein: 22g | Fats: 12g | Fiber: 4g | Sugar: 4g

---

Balsamic Glazed Lamb Loin

Preparation Time: 10 minutes | Cooking Time: 20 minutes | Portion Size: 4 servings

Ingredients:

For the Balsamic Glaze:

- 1/4 cup balsamic vinegar
- 2 tablespoons honey or a sugar substitute (optional)
- 2 cloves garlic, minced
- 1 teaspoon dried rosemary
- Salt and pepper to taste

For the Lamb Loin:

- 1,5 pounds lamb loin, trimmed and cut into 4 portions
- 2 tablespoons olive oil
- Salt and pepper to taste

Instructions:

1. In a small saucepan, combine the balsamic vinegar, honey (if using), minced garlic, dried rosemary, salt, and pepper. Bring the mixture to a gentle simmer over medium heat.

2. Reduce the heat to low and simmer for about 5-7 minutes until the glaze thickens and coats the back of a spoon. Remove it from heat and set it aside.

3. Season the lamb loin portions with salt and pepper.

4. Heat the olive oil in a large skillet over medium-high heat.

5. Add the lamb loin portions to the skillet and sear them for about 3-4 minutes per side, or until they develop a golden-brown crust. Adjust the cooking time for your preferred level of doneness.

6. During the last few minutes of cooking, brush each side of the lamb loin with the prepared balsamic glaze.

7. Remove the lamb loin from the skillet and let it rest for a few minutes before slicing.

8. Drizzle any remaining balsamic glaze over the sliced lamb loin portions before serving.

Nutritional Data (per serving):

Calories: 350 | Carbohydrates: 7g | Protein: 25g | Fats: 24g | Fiber: 0g | Sugar: 6g

Quick BBQ Pulled Pork Lettuce Wraps

Preparation Time: 15 minutes | Cooking Time: 4 hours (slow cooker) | Portion Size: 4 servings

Ingredients:

For the BBQ Pulled Pork:

- 2 pounds of boneless pork shoulder or pork butt
- 1 cup sugar-free BBQ sauce
- 1/4 cup apple cider vinegar
- 2 cloves garlic, minced
- 1 onion, chopped
- 1 teaspoon smoked paprika
- Salt and pepper to taste

For Assembly:

- 1 head of iceberg lettuce, leaves separated
- Coleslaw mix (optional, for garnish)

Instructions:

1. Place the boneless pork shoulder or pork butt in a slow cooker.
2. In a bowl, combine the sugar-free BBQ sauce, apple cider vinegar, minced garlic, chopped onion, smoked paprika, salt, and pepper. Mix well.
3. Pour the BBQ sauce mixture over the pork in the slow cooker, ensuring it's evenly coated.
4. Cover the slow cooker and cook on low for approximately 4-6 hours or until the pork is tender and easily shreds with a fork.
5. Once the pork is done, remove it from the slow cooker and shred it using two forks.
6. Return the shredded pork to the BBQ sauce mixture in the slow cooker, stirring to combine. Keep it warm until ready to serve.
7. To assemble the Quick BBQ Pulled Pork Lettuce Wraps, place a spoonful of the pulled pork mixture into each iceberg lettuce leaf.
8. Garnish with coleslaw mix if desired.

Nutritional Data (per serving, without coleslaw):

Calories: 350 | Carbohydrates: 15g | Protein: 30g | Fats: 18g | Fiber: 3g | Sugar: 3g

Garlic & Herb Marinated Beef Skewers

Preparation Time: 15 minutes | Cooking Time: 10 minutes | Portion Size: 4 servings

Ingredients:

For the Garlic & Herb Marinade:

- 1/4 cup olive oil
- 3 cloves garlic, minced
- 2 tablespoons fresh parsley, chopped
- 1 tablespoon fresh rosemary, minced
- 1 tablespoon fresh thyme, minced
- Zest of 1 lemon
- Salt and pepper to taste

For the Beef Skewers:

- 1,5 pounds beef sirloin or top sirloin, cut into 1-inch cubes
- Wooden skewers, soaked in water for 30 minutes

Instructions:

1. In a bowl, whisk together the olive oil, minced garlic, chopped fresh parsley, minced fresh rosemary, minced fresh thyme, lemon zest, salt, and pepper to create the marinade.
2. Place the beef cubes in a zip-top bag or a shallow dish, and pour the marinade over them. Seal the bag or cover the dish, then refrigerate for at least 30 minutes to marinate the beef.
3. Preheat your grill to medium-high heat.
4. Thread the marinated beef cubes onto the soaked wooden skewers, evenly distributing them.
5. Grill the beef skewers for approximately 3-5 minutes per side, or until they reach your desired level of doneness.

6. Remove the skewers from the grill and let them rest for a few minutes before serving.

Nutritional Data (per serving):

Calories: 320 | Carbohydrates: 1g | Protein: 28g | Fats: 23g | Fiber: 0g | Sugar: 0g

---

Spicy Honey Garlic Pork Bites

Preparation Time: 15 minutes | Cooking Time: 15 minutes | Portion Size: 4 servings

Ingredients:

For the Spicy Honey Garlic Sauce:

- 1/4 cup honey
- 2 tablespoons reduced-sodium soy sauce
- 2 cloves garlic, minced
- 1 teaspoon sriracha sauce (adjust to your spice preference)
- 1/2 teaspoon ground ginger
- Salt and pepper to taste

For the Pork Bites:

- 1 pound boneless pork loin, cut into bite-sized pieces
- 2 tablespoons olive oil
- 2 green onions, thinly sliced (for garnish)
- Sesame seeds (for garnish, optional)

Instructions:

1. In a small bowl, whisk together the honey, reduced-sodium soy sauce, minced garlic, sriracha sauce, ground ginger, salt, and pepper to create the Spicy Honey Garlic Sauce. Set aside.
2. Heat the olive oil in a large skillet over medium-high heat.
3. Add the bite-sized pieces of pork loin to the skillet and cook for about 3-4 minutes per side until they develop a golden-brown crust and are cooked through.
4. Pour the Spicy Honey Garlic Sauce over the cooked pork bites in the skillet.
5. Toss the pork bites in the sauce until they are evenly coated and the sauce has thickened slightly about 2-3 minutes.
6. Remove the skillet from heat.
7. To serve, garnish the Spicy Honey Garlic Pork Bites with thinly sliced green onions and sesame seeds if desired.

Nutritional Data (per serving):

Calories: 280 | Carbohydrates: 21g | Protein: 20g | Fats: 13g | Fiber: 0g | Sugar: 19g

A Voyage Through the Ocean's Bounty

Salutations once again, valued reader, and prepare yourself for an immersive journey as the waves of "The Galveston Diet for Beginners" gently usher us into the mesmerizing underwater realm of fish and seafood. This chapter is not merely an assortment of recipes but a finely curated odyssey where the ocean's bountiful treasures unveil their culinary and nutritional elegance.

With me as your devoted navigator, we shall set sail into the expansive blue, where every recipe is an island of flavors, a sanctuary where the tender, succulent textures of seafood and the enlightening essence of the Galveston diet merge in a dance of waves and wellness.

The Ocean's Melody
Dive into the depths where fish, shrimp, scallops, and a diverse medley of seafood await, each a symphony of the ocean's song, harmonizing the crisp, refreshing melodies of the sea with the warmth of gourmet artistry. Every bite is a crescendo, unveiling layers of flavors, each note echoing the profound mystery and beauty of the deep blue.

Nourished by the Sea, Guided by Galveston
With the Galveston diet as our compass, we embrace the ocean's nourishment with reverence and artistry. Each recipe is a meticulous alchemy of the sea's nutritional abundance and the diet's holistic principles. Anticipate a world where omega-rich fishes and succulent seafood are adorned with herbs and spices, each dish a balanced harmony of taste and nutrients.

A Dance of Tides and Tastes
As we drift through this chapter, every recipe is an ebb and flow of tides and tastes. Visualize the colorful coral gardens, where seafood, not just satiates but delights, each recipe echoing the dynamic dance of waves, capturing the essence of the ocean's rhythm and the Galveston diet's nutritional symphony.

Casting the Nets of Discovery
Are you ready, dear sojourner, to cast the nets of discovery into the illustrious waters where fish and seafood recipes are not mere preparations but narrations, each telling tales of the ocean's depths, the sun's kiss, the moon's embrace, all while basking in the holistic warmth of the Galveston diet?

With a spirit as boundless as the ocean and a heart as warm as the golden sands, I extend my hand, inviting you to embark upon a voyage where every recipe is a lighthouse, illuminating the paths of flavor, nutrition, and the serene waters of holistic well-being.

Lemon Garlic Shrimp Skillet

Preparation Time: 10 minutes | Cooking Time: 10 minutes | Portion Size: 4 servings

Ingredients:

- 1 pound large shrimp, peeled and deveined
- 2 tablespoons olive oil
- 4 cloves garlic, minced
- Zest of 1 lemon
- Juice of 1 lemon
- 1/4 cup low-sodium chicken broth
- 2 tablespoons fresh parsley, chopped
- Salt and pepper to taste

Instructions:

1. Season the peeled and deveined shrimp with salt, pepper, and lemon zest.
2. In a large skillet, heat the olive oil over medium-high heat.
3. Add the minced garlic to the skillet and sauté for about 30 seconds until fragrant.
4. Place the seasoned shrimp in the skillet and cook for approximately 2-3 minutes per side until they turn pink and opaque. Remove the cooked shrimp from the skillet and set them aside.
5. In the same skillet, add the lemon juice and low-sodium chicken broth. Bring the mixture to a simmer and let it cook for about 2-3 minutes, allowing it to reduce and thicken slightly.
6. Return the cooked shrimp to the skillet, tossing them in the lemon garlic sauce to coat.
7. Sprinkle chopped fresh parsley over the shrimp.
8. Serve the Lemon Garlic Shrimp Skillet immediately.

Nutritional Data (per serving):

Calories: 170 | Carbohydrates: 3g | Protein: 24g | Fats: 7g | Fiber: 0g | Sugar: 0g

Zesty Lime Grilled Salmon

Preparation Time: 15 minutes | Cooking Time: 12 minutes | Portion Size: 4 servings

Ingredients:

- 4 salmon fillets (approximately 6 ounces each)
- 2 tablespoons olive oil
- Zest of 2 limes
- Juice of 2 limes
- 2 cloves garlic, minced
- 1 teaspoon chili powder
- Salt and pepper to taste
- Fresh cilantro leaves, chopped (for garnish)

Instructions:

1. Preheat your grill to medium-high heat.
2. In a bowl, combine the olive oil, lime zest, lime juice, minced garlic, chili powder, salt, and pepper to create a zesty marinade.
3. Place the salmon fillets in a shallow dish and pour the marinade over them. Ensure the

fillets are well-coated. Marinate for at least 10 minutes, turning once.

4. Grease the grill grates to prevent sticking.
5. Place the marinated salmon fillets on the preheated grill, skin-side down.
6. Grill the salmon for approximately 4-6 minutes per side, or until it flakes easily with a fork and has grill marks.
7. Remove the grilled salmon from the heat.
8. Garnish with chopped fresh cilantro leaves.

Nutritional Data (per serving):

Calories: 280 | Carbohydrates: 2g | Protein: 32g | Fats: 15g | Fiber: 0g | Sugar: 0g

Spicy Tuna & Avocado Wrap

Preparation Time: 10 minutes | Cooking Time: 0 minutes | Portion Size: 2 wraps

Ingredients:

- 1 can (5 ounces) tuna in water, drained
- 2 tablespoons mayonnaise or Greek yogurt (for a healthier option)
- 1 teaspoon sriracha sauce (adjust to your spice preference)
- 1/2 avocado, thinly sliced
- 2 whole wheat or lettuce leaves (such as iceberg or Romaine)
- 1 small cucumber, thinly sliced
- 1/4 red onion, thinly sliced
- Salt and pepper to taste

Instructions:

1. In a bowl, combine the drained tuna, mayonnaise or Greek yogurt, and sriracha sauce. Mix well to create a spicy tuna filling.
2. Lay out two whole wheat or lettuce leaves on a clean surface.
3. Spread the spicy tuna filling evenly onto each leaf.
4. Arrange the thinly sliced avocado, cucumber, and red onion on top of the tuna.
5. Season with a pinch of salt and pepper to taste.

6. Carefully fold the sides of each leaf and roll them up, creating two wraps.
7. Secure each wrap with toothpicks if needed.
8. Slice each wrap in half diagonally and serve.

Nutritional Data (per serving - 1 wrap):

Calories: 280 | Carbohydrates: 11g | Protein: 15g | Fats: 19g | Fiber: 5g | Sugar: 2g

Herbed Cod & Veggie Bake

Preparation Time: 15 minutes | Cooking Time: 25 minutes | Portion Size: 4 servings

Ingredients:

- 4 cod fillets (approximately 6 ounces each)
- 2 cups mixed vegetables (e.g., broccoli, bell peppers, carrots), cut into bite-sized pieces
- 2 tablespoons olive oil
- 2 cloves garlic, minced
- 1 teaspoon dried thyme
- 1 teaspoon dried rosemary
- 1 teaspoon dried oregano
- Salt and pepper to taste
- Lemon wedges (for garnish, optional)

Instructions:

1. Preheat your oven to 375°F (190°C).
2. In a large mixing bowl, toss the mixed vegetables with olive oil, minced garlic, dried thyme, dried rosemary, dried oregano, salt, and pepper until they are evenly coated.
3. Place the seasoned vegetables in a baking dish in an even layer.
4. Season the cod fillets with salt and pepper and arrange them on top of the vegetables in the baking dish.
5. Cover the baking dish with aluminum foil.
6. Bake in the preheated oven for approximately 20-25 minutes, or until the cod is opaque and flakes easily with a fork.
7. Remove the foil and broil for an additional 2-3 minutes until the cod develops a light golden crust.
8. Garnish with lemon wedges if desired.

Nutritional Data (per serving):

Calories: 220 | Carbohydrates: 7g | Protein: 27g | Fats: 10g | Fiber: 3g | Sugar: 2g

---

Chili Lime Shrimp Tacos

Preparation Time: 15 minutes | Cooking Time: 5 minutes | Portion Size: 4 servings (2 tacos per serving)

Ingredients:

For the Chili Lime Shrimp:

- 1 pound large shrimp, peeled and deveined
- 2 tablespoons olive oil
- Zest of 2 limes
- Juice of 2 limes
- 2 cloves garlic, minced
- 1 teaspoon chili powder
- Salt and pepper to taste

For Assembly:

- 8 small whole wheat or corn tortillas
- 2 cups coleslaw mix (shredded cabbage and carrots)
- 1/2 cup Greek yogurt or sour cream (for topping)
- Fresh cilantro leaves (for garnish)
- Lime wedges (for garnish)

Instructions:

1. In a bowl, combine the peeled and deveined shrimp with olive oil, lime zest, lime juice, minced garlic, chili powder, salt, and pepper. Toss to coat the shrimp in the marinade.
2. Preheat a skillet over medium-high heat. Add the marinated shrimp and cook for approximately 2-3 minutes per side or until they turn pink and opaque. Remove from heat.
3. Warm the tortillas according to package instructions.
4. To assemble each taco, place a spoonful of coleslaw mix on a tortilla, followed by a few chili lime shrimp.

5. Drizzle with Greek yogurt or sour cream and garnish with fresh cilantro leaves.
6. Serve the Chili Lime Shrimp Tacos with lime wedges for an extra burst of flavor.

Nutritional Data (per serving - 2 tacos):

Calories: 330 | Carbohydrates: 31g | Protein: 25g | Fats: 12g | Fiber: 6g | Sugar: 3g

---

Quick-Seared Tuna Steaks

Preparation Time: 10 minutes | Cooking Time: 4 minutes | Portion Size: 4 servings

Ingredients:

- 4 tuna steaks (approximately 6 ounces each)
- 2 tablespoons olive oil
- 1 tablespoon sesame oil
- 2 tablespoons low-sodium soy sauce
- 1 teaspoon grated fresh ginger
- 2 cloves garlic, minced
- Salt and pepper to taste
- Sesame seeds (for garnish, optional)
- Sliced green onions (for garnish, optional)

Instructions:

1. Pat the tuna steaks dry with paper towels and season them with salt and pepper.
2. In a bowl, whisk together the olive oil, sesame oil, low-sodium soy sauce, grated fresh ginger, and minced garlic to create the marinade.
3. Place the tuna steaks in a shallow dish and pour the marinade over them. Ensure the steaks are well-coated. Marinate for at least 10 minutes, turning once.
4. Heat a skillet or grill pan over high heat until it's very hot.
5. Remove the tuna steaks from the marinade and sear them in the hot skillet or grill pan for approximately 1-2 minutes per side for rare, or adjust the cooking time for your desired level of doneness.
6. Remove the seared tuna steaks from the heat and let them rest for a few minutes.

7. Garnish with sesame seeds and sliced green onions if desired.

Nutritional Data (per serving):

Calories: 270 | Carbohydrates: 2g | Protein: 31g | Fats: 14g | Fiber: 0g | Sugar: 0g

---

Garlic Butter Scallops Deluxe

Preparation Time: 10 minutes | Cooking Time: 5 minutes | Portion Size: 4 servings

Ingredients:

- 1 pound large scallops
- 2 tablespoons olive oil
- 3 cloves garlic, minced
- 2 tablespoons unsalted butter
- Juice of 1 lemon
- 2 tablespoons fresh parsley, chopped
- Salt and pepper to taste

Instructions:

1. Pat the scallops dry with paper towels and season them with salt and pepper.
2. In a large skillet, heat the olive oil over medium-high heat.
3. Add the seasoned scallops to the skillet, ensuring they are in a single layer and not overcrowded. Sear for about 1-2 minutes per side until they develop a golden-brown crust. Work in batches if necessary.
4. Remove the seared scallops from the skillet and set them aside.
5. In the same skillet, melt the unsalted butter over medium heat.
6. Add the minced garlic and sauté for about 1 minute until fragrant.
7. Return the seared scallops to the skillet and drizzle with lemon juice.
8. Toss the scallops in the garlic butter sauce for about 1-2 minutes until they are heated through and coated with the sauce.
9. Sprinkle chopped fresh parsley over the scallops.
10. Serve the Garlic Butter Scallops Deluxe immediately.

Nutritional Data (per serving):

Calories: 220 | Carbohydrates: 4g | Protein: 18g | Fats: 14g | Fiber: 0g | Sugar: 0g

---

Honey Mustard Baked Salmon

Preparation Time: 10 minutes | Cooking Time: 15 minutes | Portion Size: 4 servings

Ingredients:

- 4 salmon fillets (approximately 6 ounces each)
- 2 tablespoons Dijon mustard
- 2 tablespoons honey
- 1 tablespoon olive oil
- 2 cloves garlic, minced
- 1 teaspoon dried dill
- Salt and pepper to taste
- Lemon wedges (for garnish, optional)

Instructions:

1. Preheat your oven to 375°F (190°C). Line a baking sheet with parchment paper or lightly grease it.
2. In a small bowl, whisk together Dijon mustard, honey, olive oil, minced garlic, dried dill, salt, and pepper to create the honey mustard glaze.
3. Place the salmon fillets on the prepared baking sheet.
4. Brush the honey mustard glaze over the top of each salmon fillet, ensuring they are evenly coated.
5. Bake the salmon in the preheated oven for approximately 12-15 minutes, or until the salmon flakes easily with a fork and has a golden-brown glaze on top.
6. Remove the baked salmon from the oven.
7. Garnish with lemon wedges and fresh dill sprigs if desired.

Nutritional Data (per serving):

Calories: 330 | Carbohydrates: 10g | Protein: 34g | Fats: 16g | Fiber: 0g | Sugar: 9g

Cajun Spiced Tilapia Fillets

Preparation Time: 10 minutes | Cooking Time: 10 minutes | Portion Size: 4 servings

Ingredients:

- 4 tilapia fillets (approximately 6 ounces each)
- 2 tablespoons olive oil
- 1 tablespoon Cajun seasoning (store-bought or homemade)
- 1 teaspoon paprika
- 1/2 teaspoon garlic powder
- 1/2 teaspoon onion powder
- 1/2 teaspoon dried thyme
- Salt and pepper to taste
- Lemon wedges (for garnish, optional)
- Fresh parsley leaves (for garnish, optional)

Instructions:

1. In a small bowl, combine Cajun seasoning, paprika, garlic powder, onion powder, dried thyme, salt, and pepper to create the Cajun spice blend.
2. Pat the tilapia fillets dry with paper towels.
3. Sprinkle the Cajun spice blend evenly over both sides of each tilapia fillet, pressing the spices onto the fish to adhere.
4. In a skillet, heat the olive oil over medium-high heat.
5. Place the seasoned tilapia fillets in the skillet and cook for approximately 3-4 minutes per side, or until the fish flakes easily with a fork and has a crispy exterior.
6. Remove the cooked Cajun Spiced Tilapia Fillets from the skillet.
7. Garnish with lemon wedges and fresh parsley leaves if desired.

Nutritional Data (per serving):

Calories: 220 | Carbohydrates: 2g | Protein: 36g | Fats: 7g | Fiber: 1g | Sugar: 0g

Paprika Lemon Butter Clams

Preparation Time: 15 minutes | Cooking Time: 10 minutes | Portion Size: 4 servings

Ingredients:

- 2 pounds fresh clams, cleaned and scrubbed
- 2 tablespoons unsalted butter
- 2 cloves garlic, minced
- 1 teaspoon smoked paprika
- Zest of 1 lemon
- Juice of 1 lemon
- 1/4 cup fresh parsley, chopped
- Salt and pepper to taste

Instructions:

1. In a large bowl, fill with cold water and add the cleaned clams. Allow them to soak for about 10 minutes to remove any sand or grit. Drain and rinse thoroughly.

2. In a large skillet or pan with a lid, melt the unsalted butter over medium-high heat.

3. Add the minced garlic and smoked paprika to the melted butter. Sauté for about 1 minute until the garlic becomes fragrant.

4. Add the cleaned clams to the skillet and toss to coat them in the garlic butter mixture.

5. Pour in the lemon juice and lemon zest over the clams.

6. Cover the skillet with a lid and cook for approximately 5-7 minutes, or until the clams have opened. Discard any clams that do not open.

7. Season with salt and pepper to taste, and sprinkle fresh parsley over the cooked clams.

8. Serve the Paprika Lemon Butter Clams in shallow bowls, drizzling the flavorful broth over the top.

Nutritional Data (per serving):

Calories: 160 | Carbohydrates: 6g | Protein: 10g | Fats: 10g | Fiber: 0g | Sugar: 0g

Sweet Chili Shrimp Stir-Fry

Preparation Time: 15 minutes | Cooking Time: 10 minutes | Portion Size: 4 servings

Ingredients:

For the Sweet Chili Sauce:

- 1/4 cup low-sodium soy sauce
- 2 tablespoons rice vinegar
- 2 tablespoons honey
- 1 tablespoon Sriracha sauce (adjust to your spice preference)
- 1 teaspoon cornstarch

For the Stir-Fry:

- 1 pound large shrimp, peeled and deveined
- 2 tablespoons olive oil
- 3 cups mixed vegetables (e.g., bell peppers, snap peas, broccoli), sliced
- 3 cloves garlic, minced
- 1 teaspoon fresh ginger, minced

- Salt and pepper to taste
- Cooked brown rice or cauliflower rice (for serving)

Instructions:

1. In a small bowl, whisk together the soy sauce, rice vinegar, honey, Sriracha sauce, and cornstarch to create the sweet chili sauce. Set aside.

2. Pat the peeled and deveined shrimp dry with paper towels and season them with salt and pepper.

3. Heat 1 tablespoon of olive oil in a large skillet or wok over medium-high heat.

4. Add the seasoned shrimp to the skillet and cook for 2-3 minutes per side or until they turn pink and opaque. Remove the shrimp from the skillet and set them aside.

5. In the same skillet, add the remaining 1 tablespoon of olive oil.

6. Add the minced garlic and minced ginger, and sauté for about 1 minute until fragrant.

7. Add the sliced mixed vegetables to the skillet and stir-fry for approximately 4-5 minutes, or until they are tender-crisp.

8. Return the cooked shrimp to the skillet.

9. Pour the sweet chili sauce over the shrimp and vegetables. Stir-fry for an additional 2 minutes until everything is heated through and coated with the sauce.

10. Serve the Sweet Chili Shrimp Stir-Fry over cooked brown rice or cauliflower rice.

Nutritional Data (per serving, excluding rice):

Calories: 230 | Carbohydrates: 15g | Protein: 24g | Fats: 8g | Fiber: 3g | Sugar: 8g

Pesto Grilled Swordfish

Preparation Time: 15 minutes | Cooking Time: 10 minutes | Portion Size: 4 servings

Ingredients:

- 4 swordfish steaks (approximately 6 ounces each)
- 1/2 cup fresh basil leaves
- 2 cloves garlic
- 1/4 cup grated Parmesan cheese
- 2 tablespoons pine nuts
- 1/4 cup olive oil
- Salt and pepper to taste
- Lemon wedges (for garnish, optional)

Instructions:

1. Preheat your grill to medium-high heat.
2. In a food processor, combine fresh basil leaves, garlic, grated Parmesan cheese, pine nuts, and olive oil. Blend until you have a smooth pesto sauce. Season with salt and pepper to taste.
3. Pat the swordfish steaks dry with paper towels.
4. Brush one side of each swordfish steak with the prepared pesto sauce.
5. Place the swordfish steaks on the preheated grill, pesto-side down.
6. Grill for approximately 4-5 minutes on each side, or until the swordfish is opaque and flakes easily with a fork. The internal temperature should reach 145°F (63°C).
7. Remove the grilled swordfish from the grill and let it rest for a few minutes.
8. Garnish with lemon wedges if desired.

Nutritional Data (per serving):

Calories: 350 | Carbohydrates: 2g | Protein: 36g | Fats: 23g | Fiber: 1g | Sugar: 0g

Sesame Seared Salmon

Preparation Time: 10 minutes | Cooking Time: 8 minutes | Portion Size: 4 servings

Ingredients:

- 4 salmon fillets (approximately 6 ounces each)
- 2 tablespoons sesame seeds
- 2 tablespoons black sesame seeds
- 1 teaspoon olive oil
- 2 tablespoons low-sodium soy sauce
- 1 teaspoon honey
- 1 teaspoon grated fresh ginger
- 2 cloves garlic, minced
- Salt and pepper to taste
- Fresh cilantro leaves (for garnish, optional)
- Lemon wedges (for garnish, optional)

Instructions:

1. Pat the salmon fillets dry with paper towels.
2. In a shallow dish, combine sesame seeds and black sesame seeds.
3. Brush each salmon fillet with olive oil and season with salt and pepper.
4. Press each side of the salmon fillets into the sesame seed mixture to coat them evenly.
5. Heat a skillet over medium-high heat.
6. Place the sesame-coated salmon fillets in the skillet and cook for approximately 3-4 minutes per side, or until they are golden brown on the outside and cooked to your desired level of doneness.
7. While the salmon is cooking, prepare the sauce. In a small bowl, whisk together low-sodium soy sauce, honey, grated fresh ginger, and minced garlic.
8. Once the salmon is done, remove it from the skillet.
9. Drizzle the sauce over the sesame seared salmon.
10. Garnish with fresh cilantro leaves and lemon wedges if desired.

Nutritional Data (per serving):

Calories: 330 | Carbohydrates: 7g | Protein: 34g | Fats: 19g | Fiber: 2g | Sugar: 2g

Curry Shrimp & Coconut Rice

Preparation Time: 15 minutes | Cooking Time: 25 minutes | Portion Size: 4 servings

Ingredients:

For the Curry Shrimp:

- 1 pound large shrimp, peeled and deveined
- 2 tablespoons olive oil
- 1 onion, finely chopped
- 2 cloves garlic, minced
- 2 tablespoons curry powder
- 1 can (14 ounces) diced tomatoes
- 1 can (14 ounces) coconut milk
- Salt and pepper to taste
- Fresh cilantro leaves (for garnish, optional)

For the Coconut Rice:

- 1 cup long-grain white rice
- 1 can (14 ounces) coconut milk
- 1/2 cup water
- 1/2 teaspoon salt

Instructions:

For the Coconut Rice:

1. In a medium saucepan, combine the white rice, coconut milk, water, and salt.
2. Bring the mixture to a boil over medium-high heat.
3. Reduce the heat to low, cover, and simmer for 15-20 minutes, or until the rice is tender and the liquid is absorbed.
4. Remove the saucepan from heat and let it sit, covered, for an additional 5 minutes. Fluff the rice with a fork.

For the Curry Shrimp:

1. In a large skillet, heat 2 tablespoons of olive oil over medium-high heat.
2. Add the finely chopped onion and sauté for about 2-3 minutes, or until it becomes translucent.
3. Stir in the minced garlic and curry powder. Cook for an additional minute to toast the spices.
4. Add the peeled and deveined shrimp to the skillet. Cook for 2-3 minutes per side, or until the shrimp turn pink and opaque. Remove the cooked shrimp from the skillet and set them aside.
5. In the same skillet, add the diced tomatoes and coconut milk. Bring the mixture to a simmer.
6. Simmer for 5-7 minutes, stirring occasionally, until the sauce thickens.
7. Return the cooked shrimp to the skillet and heat through for another 2 minutes. Season with salt and pepper to taste.

To Serve:

1. Spoon a portion of the coconut rice onto each plate.
2. Top the rice with the flavorful Curry Shrimp and sauce.
3. Garnish with fresh cilantro leaves if desired.

Nutritional Data (per serving):

Calories: 520 | Carbohydrates: 44g | Protein: 20g | Fats: 32g | Fiber: 3g | Sugar: 4g

Lemon Herb Shrimp & Asparagus

Preparation Time: 15 minutes | Cooking Time: 10 minutes | Portion Size: 4 servings

Ingredients:

- 1 pound large shrimp, peeled and deveined
- 1 bunch fresh asparagus spears, trimmed and cut into 2-inch pieces
- 2 tablespoons olive oil
- 2 cloves garlic, minced
- Zest of 1 lemon
- Juice of 1 lemon
- 1 tablespoon fresh thyme leaves
- Salt and pepper to taste
- Fresh parsley leaves (for garnish, optional)

Instructions:

1. In a bowl, combine the peeled and deveined shrimp with olive oil, minced garlic, lemon zest, fresh thyme leaves, salt, and pepper. Toss to coat the shrimp evenly and let them marinate for about 10 minutes.
2. While the shrimp are marinating, heat a large skillet over medium-high heat.
3. Add the marinated shrimp to the hot skillet and cook for approximately 2-3 minutes per side, or until they turn pink and opaque. Remove the cooked shrimp from the skillet and set them aside.
4. In the same skillet, add the trimmed asparagus pieces and cook for about 4-5 minutes, or until they become tender-crisp.
5. Return the cooked shrimp to the skillet with the asparagus.
6. Pour the lemon juice over the shrimp and asparagus. Stir to combine and heat for an additional minute until everything is well-coated and heated through.
7. Season with additional salt and pepper if needed.

8. Garnish with fresh parsley leaves if desired.

Nutritional Data (per serving):

Calories: 180 | Carbohydrates: 6g | Protein: 24g | Fats: 7g | Fiber: 3g | Sugar: 2g

Grilled White Fish with Mango Salsa

Preparation Time: 15 minutes | Cooking Time: 10 minutes | Portion Size: 4 servings

Ingredients:

For the Grilled White Fish:

- 4 white fish fillets (such as cod, snapper, or tilapia), approximately 6 ounces each
- 2 tablespoons olive oil
- 1 teaspoon ground cumin
- 1 teaspoon smoked paprika
- Salt and pepper to taste

For the Mango Salsa:

- 2 ripe mangoes, peeled, pitted, and diced
- 1/2 red onion, finely chopped
- 1 red bell pepper, diced
- 1/4 cup fresh cilantro, chopped
- Juice of 2 limes
- Salt and pepper to taste

Instructions:

1. Preheat your grill to medium-high heat.
2. In a small bowl, combine olive oil, ground cumin, smoked paprika, salt, and pepper.
3. Brush both sides of the white fish fillets with the spice-infused olive oil mixture.
4. Place the seasoned fish fillets on the preheated grill and cook for approximately 4-5 minutes per side, or until the fish is opaque and flakes easily with a fork.
5. While the fish is grilling, prepare the mango salsa. In a bowl, combine diced mangoes, finely chopped red onion, diced red bell pepper, fresh cilantro, lime juice, salt, and pepper. Toss everything together until well mixed.

6. Once the white fish is done grilling, remove it from the grill and let it rest for a few minutes.
7. Serve the Grilled White Fish with Mango Salsa on individual plates, topping each fillet with a generous spoonful of the flavorful mango salsa.

Nutritional Data (per serving):

Calories: 260 | Carbohydrates: 29g | Protein: 30g | Fats: 6g | Fiber: 4g | Sugar: 23g

Pan-Seared Scallops & Pea Puree

Preparation Time: 15 minutes | Cooking Time: 10 minutes | Portion Size: 4 servings

Ingredients:

For the Pan-Seared Scallops:

- 1 pound large sea scallops
- 1 tablespoon olive oil
- Salt and pepper to taste
- Fresh lemon wedges (for garnish, optional)

For the Pea Puree:

- 2 cups frozen peas, thawed
- 1/4 cup fresh mint leaves
- 2 cloves garlic, minced
- 1/4 cup low-sodium chicken or vegetable broth
- 1 tablespoon olive oil
- Salt and pepper to taste

Instructions:

1. Start by making the Pea Puree: a. In a microwave-safe bowl, steam the thawed peas according to the package instructions. b. In a food processor, combine the steamed peas, fresh mint leaves, minced garlic, chicken or vegetable broth, and olive oil. c. Process until you have a smooth and creamy pea puree. Season with salt and pepper to taste. Set aside.
2. Pat the sea scallops dry with paper towels to remove any excess moisture.

3. Heat 1 tablespoon of olive oil in a large skillet over medium-high heat.
4. Season both sides of the scallops with salt and pepper.
5. Carefully add the seasoned scallops to the hot skillet, making sure they are not overcrowded. Sear for approximately 2-3 minutes on each side, or until they develop a golden crust and are opaque in the center.
6. To serve, spoon a generous portion of the pea puree onto each plate.
7. Arrange the pan-seared scallops on top of the pea puree.
8. Garnish with fresh lemon wedges if desired.

Nutritional Data (per serving):

Calories: 220 | Carbohydrates: 14g | Protein: 20g | Fats: 9g | Fiber: 5g | Sugar: 4g

Spiced Mackerel with Cucumber Salad

Preparation Time: 15 minutes | Cooking Time: 10 minutes | Portion Size: 4 servings

Ingredients:

For the Spiced Mackerel:

- 4 mackerel fillets (approximately 6 ounces each)
- 1 teaspoon ground cumin
- 1 teaspoon ground coriander
- 1/2 teaspoon smoked paprika
- 1/2 teaspoon ground turmeric
- 1/2 teaspoon ground cinnamon
- Salt and pepper to taste
- 2 tablespoons olive oil

For the Cucumber Salad:

- 2 cucumbers, thinly sliced
- 1 red onion, thinly sliced
- 1/4 cup fresh cilantro, chopped
- Juice of 2 limes
- 2 tablespoons extra-virgin olive oil
- Salt and pepper to taste

Instructions:

1. In a small bowl, combine ground cumin, ground coriander, smoked paprika, ground turmeric, ground cinnamon, salt, and pepper.
2. Season both sides of the mackerel fillet with the spice mixture.
3. Heat 2 tablespoons of olive oil in a skillet over medium-high heat.
4. Add the seasoned mackerel fillets to the hot skillet and cook for approximately 3-4 minutes per side, or until they are golden brown and cooked through. The internal temperature should reach 145°F (63°C).
5. While the mackerel is cooking, prepare the cucumber salad. In a large bowl, combine thinly sliced cucumbers, thinly sliced red onion, chopped fresh cilantro, lime juice, extra-virgin olive oil, salt, and pepper. Toss everything together until well mixed.
6. Once the mackerel is done, remove it from the skillet.
7. Serve the Spiced Mackerel with Cucumber Salad on individual plates, with a generous serving of the refreshing cucumber salad alongside the flavorful fish.

Nutritional Data (per serving):

Calories: 340 | Carbohydrates: 10g | Protein: 32g | Fats: 20g | Fiber: 2g | Sugar: 4g

---

One-Pan Lemon Pepper Tilapia

Preparation Time: 10 minutes | Cooking Time: 20 minutes | Portion Size: 4 servings

Ingredients:

- 4 tilapia fillets (approximately 6 ounces each)
- 2 tablespoons olive oil
- 2 teaspoons lemon pepper seasoning
- 1 lemon, thinly sliced
- 1/4 cup fresh parsley, chopped
- Salt and pepper to taste

Instructions:

1. Preheat your oven to 375°F (190°C).
2. Pat the tilapia fillets dry with paper towels and place them on a plate.
3. Drizzle olive oil over both sides of each tilapia fillet, then sprinkle lemon pepper seasoning, salt, and pepper evenly over them. Rub the seasonings into the fillets.
4. In a large ovenproof skillet, heat a bit of olive oil over medium-high heat.
5. Add the seasoned tilapia fillets to the skillet and cook for 2-3 minutes on each side, or until they are lightly browned.
6. Remove the skillet from heat and place lemon slices on top of each fillet.
7. Transfer the skillet to the preheated oven and bake for about 10-12 minutes, or until the tilapia is cooked through and flakes easily with a fork.
8. Remove the skillet from the oven, garnish the tilapia with fresh chopped parsley, and serve immediately.

Nutritional Data (per serving):

Calories: 210 | Carbohydrates: 4g | Protein: 30g | Fats: 9g | Fiber: 1g | Sugar: 1g

A Whimsical Journey into Sweet Indulgence

Beloved reader, as the pages of "The Galveston Diet for Beginners" gracefully unfold, we are beckoned into a realm where whimsy and delight dance freely, where every recipe is a tender sonnet and every bite, a celebration. Welcome to the enchanting world of desserts, a chapter not just written, but lovingly composed to echo the sweet symphony of indulgence harmonized with the melodies of wellness.

I am your humble companion, inviting you into an embrace where the tender touch of sweetness marries the profound wisdom of the Galveston diet. Here, every dessert is a crafted masterpiece, echoing the delightful convergence of pleasure and nutrition.

The Ballet of Sweetness
Visualize a world where chocolates, fruits, creams, and spices converge in a ballet of sweetness, where every recipe is a dance of flavors, tenderly waltzing to the gentle tunes of well-being. In this mesmerizing chapter, desserts are not merely the finale but an integral movement in the harmonious composition of the Galveston culinary symphony.

Galveston's Sweet Harmony
With the principles of the Galveston diet illuminating our path, each dessert is a harmonious blend of indulgence and nourishment. We embrace the art of sweet creation with ingredients that not only delight the senses but also honor the body's temple. This is a realm where the rich, decadent textures and aromas of desserts are lovingly woven with the touch of nutritional grace.

A Confluence of Stars
Prepare to traverse a starlit sky where every recipe is a constellation, a unique alignment of ingredients echoing the celestial dance of taste and well-being. Here, desserts do not just conclude a meal; they narrate the closing chapters of a culinary epic, where the sweet notes of indulgence echo the profound verses of the Galveston diet.

The Moonlit Path Awaits
Are you prepared, dear traveler, to tread the moonlit paths where desserts are not just sweet concoctions but lyrical compositions, each echoing the gentle serenade of the night, the tender kiss of the stars, and the warm embrace of the Galveston diet's nutritional wisdom?

Berries & Cream Almond Crisp

Preparation Time: 15 minutes | Cooking Time: 25 minutes | Portion Size: 6 servings

Ingredients:

For the Fruit Filling:

- 4 cups mixed berries (strawberries, blueberries, raspberries, and blackberries)
- 1/4 cup erythritol or stevia (for sweetness)
- 1 tablespoon lemon juice
- 1 teaspoon vanilla extract
- 1 tablespoon coconut flour

For the Almond Crisp Topping:

- 1 cup almond flour
- 1/2 cup sliced almonds
- 1/4 cup erythritol or stevia (for sweetness)
- 1/4 cup unsweetened shredded coconut
- 1/4 cup cold unsalted butter, cut into small pieces (or coconut oil for a dairy-free option)
- 1/2 teaspoon ground cinnamon
- A pinch of salt

For the Whipped Cream (optional):

- 1 cup heavy whipping cream
- 1 teaspoon vanilla extract
- 1 tablespoon erythritol or stevia (for sweetness)

Instructions:

For the Fruit Filling:

1. Preheat your oven to 350°F (175°C).
2. In a large mixing bowl, combine the mixed berries, erythritol (or stevia), lemon juice, vanilla extract, and coconut flour. Toss everything together until the berries are well coated.
3. Transfer the berry mixture to a 9x9-inch (23x23 cm) baking dish.

For the Almond Crisp Topping:

1. In a separate bowl, combine the almond flour, sliced almonds, erythritol (or stevia), unsweetened shredded coconut, ground cinnamon, and a pinch of salt.
2. Add the cold butter pieces (or coconut oil) to the dry mixture. Using a fork or your hands, work the butter into the dry ingredients until you have a crumbly texture.
3. Sprinkle the almond crisp topping evenly over the fruit filling in the baking dish.
4. Bake in the preheated oven for about 25 minutes, or until the topping is golden brown, and the fruit filling is bubbling.

For the Whipped Cream (optional):

1. While the crisp is baking, you can prepare the whipped cream if desired. In a mixing bowl, whip the heavy cream, vanilla extract, and erythritol (or stevia) until stiff peaks form.

To Serve:

1. Allow the Berries & Cream Almond Crisp to cool slightly before serving. Top each portion with a dollop of whipped cream if desired.

Nutritional Data (per serving, without whipped cream):

Calories: 318 | Carbohydrates: 17g | Protein: 6g | Fats: 27g | Fiber: 7g | Sugar: 4g

Chocolate Avocado Mousse Bliss

Preparation Time: 15 minutes | Cooking Time: 0 minutes | Portion Size: 4 servings

Ingredients:

- 2 ripe avocados
- 1/4 cup unsweetened cocoa powder
- 1/4 cup almond milk (unsweetened)
- 1/4 cup erythritol or stevia (for sweetness)
- 1 teaspoon vanilla extract
- A pinch of salt
- Fresh berries (for garnish, optional)

Instructions:

1. Cut the ripe avocados in half, remove the pits, and scoop out the flesh into a blender or food processor.
2. Add the unsweetened cocoa powder, almond milk, erythritol (or stevia), vanilla extract, and a pinch of salt to the blender or food processor.
3. Blend all the ingredients until smooth and creamy. You may need to stop and scrape down the sides a few times to ensure everything is well mixed.
4. Taste the mousse and adjust the sweetness or cocoa powder to your liking.
5. Once the mousse reaches your desired taste and consistency, transfer it to serving bowls or glasses.
6. Refrigerate for at least 30 minutes to chill and set.
7. Before serving, you can garnish with fresh berries if desired.

Nutritional Data (per serving, without berries):

Calories: 197 | Carbohydrates: 14g | Protein: 3g | Fats: 16g | Fiber: 8g | Sugar: 1g

Zesty Lime & Coconut Sorbet

Preparation Time: 10 minutes | Freezing Time: 4 hours | Portion Size: 4 servings

Ingredients:

- 4 limes, juiced
- Zest of 2 limes
- 1 can (14 oz) full-fat coconut milk
- 1/4 cup erythritol or stevia (for sweetness)
- 1 teaspoon vanilla extract
- A pinch of salt
- Fresh mint leaves (for garnish, optional)

Instructions:

1. In a mixing bowl, combine the freshly squeezed lime juice and lime zest.
2. Add the full-fat coconut milk, erythritol (or stevia), vanilla extract, and a pinch of salt to the lime mixture.
3. Whisk all the ingredients together until well combined.
4. Taste the mixture and adjust the sweetness if needed by adding more erythritol or stevia.
5. Pour the mixture into an ice cream maker and churn according to the manufacturer's instructions until it reaches a sorbet-like

consistency. This typically takes 20-25 minutes.

6. Transfer the sorbet to an airtight container and freeze for at least 4 hours to firm up.

7. When serving, garnish with fresh mint leaves if desired.

Nutritional Data (per serving, without garnish):

Calories: 180 | Carbohydrates: 6g | Protein: 1g | Fats: 18g | Fiber: 1g | Sugar: 0g

Almond Butter & Banana Smoothie

Preparation Time: 5 minutes | Cooking Time: 0 minutes | Portion Size: 2 servings

Ingredients:

- 2 ripe bananas
- 2 tablespoons almond butter
- 1 cup unsweetened almond milk
- 1/2 cup plain Greek yogurt
- 1 teaspoon honey or maple syrup (optional for sweetness)
- 1/2 teaspoon pure vanilla extract
- Ice cubes (optional)
- Ground cinnamon (for garnish, optional)

Instructions:

1. Peel the ripe bananas and place them in a blender.

2. Add almond butter, unsweetened almond milk, plain Greek yogurt, honey (if desired), and pure vanilla extract to the blender.

3. If you prefer a colder smoothie, you can also add a handful of ice cubes to the blender.

4. Blend all the ingredients until smooth and creamy.

5. Taste the smoothie and adjust the sweetness by adding more honey or maple syrup if needed.

6. Pour the smoothie into glasses.

7. Optionally, garnish with a sprinkle of ground cinnamon.

Nutritional Data (per serving, without optional honey or maple syrup):

Calories: 240 | Carbohydrates: 27g | Protein: 8g | Fats: 13g | Fiber: 4g | Sugar: 13g

Vanilla Berry Chia Pudding Delight

Preparation Time: 10 minutes | Cooking Time: 0 minutes | Portion Size: 2 servings

Ingredients:

- 1/4 cup chia seeds
- 1 cup unsweetened almond milk
- 1 teaspoon pure vanilla extract
- 1 tablespoon honey or maple syrup (optional for sweetness)
- 1/2 cup mixed berries (strawberries, blueberries, raspberries)
- Sliced almonds (for garnish, optional)
- Fresh mint leaves (for garnish, optional)

Instructions:

1. In a mixing bowl, combine the chia seeds and unsweetened almond milk.

2. Add the pure vanilla extract and honey (if desired) to the mixture. Stir well to combine all the ingredients.

3. Cover the bowl and refrigerate for at least 2 hours, or preferably overnight. This allows the chia seeds to absorb the liquid and create a pudding-like consistency.

4. Before serving, give the chia pudding a good stir to evenly distribute the chia seeds.

5. Wash and prepare the mixed berries. You can slice strawberries and leave the other berries whole.

6. Divide the chia pudding into two serving glasses or bowls.

7. Top each serving with the mixed berries.

8. If desired, garnish with sliced almonds and fresh mint leaves for added flavor and presentation.

Nutritional Data (per serving, without optional honey or maple syrup):

Calories: 180 | Carbohydrates: 21g | Protein: 5g | Fats: 8g | Fiber: 10g | Sugar: 7g

---

Cinnamon Spiced Baked Apples

Preparation Time: 10 minutes | Cooking Time: 30 minutes | Portion Size: 2 servings

Ingredients:

- 2 large apples (such as Honeycrisp or Granny Smith)
- 1 teaspoon ground cinnamon
- 1/4 teaspoon ground nutmeg
- 1/4 teaspoon ground cloves
- 1 tablespoon honey (optional for added sweetness)
- 2 tablespoons chopped walnuts or almonds (optional)
- Greek yogurt or low-fat vanilla yogurt (for serving, optional)

Instructions:

1. Preheat your oven to 350°F (175°C).
2. Wash the apples thoroughly and pat them dry with a paper towel.
3. Using an apple corer or a sharp knife, remove the cores and seeds from the apples, creating a cavity in the center. Leave the bottom intact to create a well for the filling.
4. In a small bowl, combine the ground cinnamon, ground nutmeg, and ground cloves. Mix well.
5. Sprinkle the cinnamon spice mixture evenly inside the cavities of the apples.
6. Place the apples in a baking dish. If you want to add extra sweetness, drizzle 1/2 tablespoon of honey into each apple.
7. Optional: Sprinkle chopped walnuts or almonds over the top of the apples for added crunch and flavor.
8. Cover the baking dish with aluminum foil and bake in the preheated oven for approximately 30 minutes or until the apples are tender. The baking time may vary depending on the size and variety of apples you use.
9. Once the apples are done baking, remove them from the oven and allow them to cool slightly.
10. Serve the cinnamon spiced baked apples warm. Optionally, you can serve them with a dollop of Greek yogurt or low-fat vanilla yogurt for a creamy contrast.

Nutritional Data (per serving, without optional honey or yogurt):

Calories: 100 | Carbohydrates: 25g | Protein: 1g | Fats: 0.5g | Fiber: 4g | Sugar: 19g

Chocolate-Dipped Strawberry Clusters

Preparation Time: 15 minutes | Cooking Time: 0 minutes | Portion Size: 2 servings

Ingredients:

- 1 cup fresh strawberries, hulled and halved
- 2 tablespoons dark chocolate chips (70% cocoa or higher)
- 1/2 teaspoon coconut oil
- 1 tablespoon chopped unsalted nuts (such as almonds or pecans)
- 1/2 teaspoon unsweetened shredded coconut (optional)
- A pinch of sea salt (optional)

Instructions:

1. Line a baking sheet or tray with parchment paper and set it aside.
2. In a microwave-safe bowl, combine the dark chocolate chips and coconut oil.
3. Microwave the chocolate in 15-second intervals, stirring each time until it's completely melted and smooth. Be careful not to overheat the chocolate.
4. Dip the cut side of each strawberry half into the melted chocolate, allowing any excess to drip back into the bowl.
5. Place the chocolate-dipped strawberry halves on the prepared baking sheet.
6. While the chocolate is still soft, sprinkle the chopped nuts over the strawberries. If desired, add a pinch of unsweetened shredded coconut and a tiny sprinkle of sea salt for added flavor.
7. Allow the chocolate to set by placing the baking sheet in the refrigerator for about 15 minutes.
8. Once the chocolate has hardened, remove the strawberry clusters from the fridge.
9. Serve the Chocolate-Dipped Strawberry Clusters as a delightful and guilt-free dessert or snack.

Nutritional Data (per serving):

Calories: 120 | Carbohydrates: 12g | Protein: 2g | Fats: 8g | Fiber: 3g | Sugar: 6g

Creamy Lemon & Berry Frozen Yogurt

Preparation Time: 10 minutes | Freezing Time: 4 hours | Portion Size: 4 servings

Ingredients:

- 2 cups plain Greek yogurt (full-fat or low-fat)
- 1/4 cup fresh lemon juice (from about 2 lemons)
- 1 tablespoon lemon zest
- 1/4 cup honey or a sugar-free sweetener (adjust to taste)
- 1 cup mixed berries (strawberries, blueberries, raspberries)

Instructions:

1. In a mixing bowl, combine the Greek yogurt, fresh lemon juice, lemon zest, and honey (or sugar-free sweetener). Mix well until everything is thoroughly combined.
2. Gently fold in the mixed berries. You can either leave them whole or chop them into smaller pieces, depending on your preference.
3. Pour the mixture into a freezer-safe container or loaf pan. Spread it out evenly.
4. Cover the container with plastic wrap or a lid and place it in the freezer.
5. Allow the frozen yogurt to freeze for at least 4 hours or until it reaches your desired consistency. You can stir it every hour or so to prevent ice crystals from forming.
6. When ready to serve, remove the frozen yogurt from the freezer and let it sit at room temperature for a few minutes to soften slightly.
7. Scoop the Creamy Lemon & Berry Frozen Yogurt into bowls or cones and enjoy this Galveston Diet-friendly treat!

Nutritional Data (per serving):

Calories: 150 | Carbohydrates: 20g | Protein: 9g | Fats: 4g | Fiber: 2g | Sugar: 16g

Almond & Cocoa Energy Bites

Preparation Time: 15 minutes | No Cooking Required | Portion Size: 12 bites

Ingredients:

- 1 cup almonds, unsalted
- 1/4 cup unsweetened cocoa powder
- 1/4 cup almond butter (no added sugar)
- 1/4 cup honey or a sugar-free sweetener
- 1 teaspoon vanilla extract
- A pinch of salt
- 1/4 cup unsweetened shredded coconut (optional, for coating)

Instructions:

1. In a food processor, combine the almonds, unsweetened cocoa powder, almond butter, honey (or sugar-free sweetener), vanilla extract, and a pinch of salt.

2. Pulse the mixture until it comes together into a sticky, dough-like consistency. You may need to scrape down the sides of the food processor and continue pulsing to ensure even mixing.

3. Once the mixture is well combined, remove it from the food processor.

4. Scoop out small portions of the mixture and roll them between your palms to form bite-sized balls.

5. If desired, roll the energy bites in unsweetened shredded coconut to add extra flavor and texture.

6. Place the Almond & Cocoa Energy Bites on a tray or plate lined with parchment paper and refrigerate them for at least 30 minutes to firm up.

7. Once the bites have hardened slightly, transfer them to an airtight container and store them in the refrigerator.

8. Enjoy these energy-packed bites whenever you need a quick, Galveston Diet-friendly snack!

Nutritional Data (per bite):

Calories: 110 | Carbohydrates: 9g | Protein: 3g | Fats: 7g | Fiber: 2g | Sugar: 6g

Vanilla Almond Panna Cotta

Preparation Time: 10 minutes | Cooking Time: 10 minutes | Chilling Time: 2 hours | Portion Size: 4 servings

Ingredients:

- 2 cups unsweetened almond milk
- 1/4 cup almond butter (no added sugar)
- 1/4 cup honey or a sugar-free sweetener
- 1 teaspoon vanilla extract
- 2 teaspoons gelatin powder
- 2 tablespoons water
- Sliced almonds and fresh berries for garnish (optional)

Instructions:

1. In a small bowl, combine the gelatin powder and 2 tablespoons of water. Stir well and let it sit for about 5 minutes to allow the gelatin to bloom.

2. In a saucepan, heat the almond milk over medium heat until it's warm but not boiling. Remove it from the heat.

3. In a separate saucepan, warm the almond butter and honey over low heat, stirring until they are well combined.

4. Add the bloomed gelatin to the warm almond milk and stir until it's completely dissolved.

5. Combine the almond milk-gelatin mixture with the almond butter-honey mixture and stir until smooth. Add the vanilla extract and mix well.

6. Pour the mixture into individual serving glasses or ramekins.

7. Refrigerate the panna cotta for at least 2 hours, or until it's set.
8. Before serving, garnish with sliced almonds and fresh berries, if desired.
9. Enjoy your Vanilla Almond Panna Cotta as a Galveston Diet-friendly dessert!

Nutritional Data (per serving):

Calories: 180 | Carbohydrates: 16g | Protein: 5g | Fats: 11g | Fiber: 1g | Sugar: 13g

Grilled Peaches with Cinnamon Drizzle

Preparation Time: 10 minutes | Cooking Time: 6 minutes | Portion Size: 4 servings

Ingredients:

- 4 ripe peaches, halved and pitted
- 1 tablespoon olive oil
- 1 teaspoon ground cinnamon
- 2 tablespoons honey or a sugar-free sweetener
- Fresh mint leaves for garnish (optional)

Instructions:

1. Preheat your grill to medium-high heat.
2. In a small bowl, mix the olive oil and ground cinnamon to create a cinnamon-infused oil.
3. Brush the cut sides of the peaches with the cinnamon-infused oil.
4. Place the peaches, cut-side down, onto the preheated grill grates.
5. Grill the peaches for about 3 minutes on each side, or until they develop grill marks and are slightly softened.
6. Remove the grilled peaches from the grill and place them on a serving platter.
7. Drizzle the honey or sugar-free sweetener over the grilled peaches.
8. Garnish with fresh mint leaves if desired.
9. Serve your Grilled Peaches with Cinnamon Drizzle as a delicious Galveston Diet-friendly dessert or snack.

Nutritional Data (per serving):

Calories: 80 | Carbohydrates: 19g | Protein: 1g | Fats: 2g | Fiber: 2g | Sugar: 17g

Honey Sweetened Dark Chocolate Mousse

Preparation Time: 15 minutes | Cooking Time: 5 minutes | Portion Size: 4 servings

Ingredients:

- 6 ounces (170g) dark chocolate (70% cocoa or higher), chopped
- 1/4 cup honey
- 1 teaspoon pure vanilla extract
- Pinch of salt
- 1 cup unsweetened coconut milk
- 2 large eggs, separated
- Fresh berries for garnish (optional)

Instructions:

1. In a heatproof bowl, combine the chopped dark chocolate, honey, pure vanilla extract, and a pinch of salt.
2. Heat the coconut milk in a saucepan over medium heat until it begins to simmer. Do not let it boil.
3. Once the coconut milk is simmering, remove it from the heat and pour it over the chocolate mixture.
4. Let the mixture sit undisturbed for 1-2 minutes to allow the chocolate to melt.
5. Gently whisk the chocolate and coconut milk mixture until smooth and well combined.
6. In a separate bowl, whisk the egg yolks until they become slightly pale.
7. Slowly whisk the egg yolks into the chocolate mixture.
8. In another bowl, whip the egg whites until stiff peaks form.
9. Carefully fold the whipped egg whites into the chocolate mixture until no streaks remain.

10. Spoon the mousse into serving glasses or bowls.
11. Chill the mousse in the refrigerator for at least 4 hours, or until it is set.
12. Garnish with fresh berries before serving, if desired.

Nutritional Data (per serving):

Calories: 320 | Carbohydrates: 34g | Protein: 4g | Fats: 19g | Fiber: 3g | Sugar: 28g

Coconut & Pineapple Ice Cream Bliss

Preparation Time: 10 minutes | Freezing Time: 4 hours | Portion Size: 4 servings

Ingredients:

- 2 cups unsweetened coconut milk
- 2 cups frozen pineapple chunks
- 1/4 cup honey
- 1 teaspoon pure vanilla extract

Instructions:

1. In a blender, combine the unsweetened coconut milk, frozen pineapple chunks, honey, and pure vanilla extract.
2. Blend until the mixture is smooth and well combined.
3. Taste the mixture and adjust the sweetness with additional honey if desired.
4. Pour the mixture into an ice cream maker and churn according to the manufacturer's instructions.
5. Once the ice cream has reached a soft-serve consistency, transfer it to a lidded container.
6. Freeze the ice cream for at least 4 hours or until firm.
7. Before serving, allow the ice cream to sit at room temperature for a few minutes to soften slightly for easier scooping.
8. Serve in small bowls or cones.

Nutritional Data (per serving):

Calories: 210 | Carbohydrates: 32g | Protein: 1g | Fats: 10g | Fiber: 2g | Sugar: 27g

Caramel Drizzled Baked Pears

Preparation Time: 10 minutes | Cooking Time: 30 minutes | Portion Size: 4 servings

Ingredients:

- 4 ripe pears, halved and cored
- 2 tablespoons unsalted butter, melted
- 2 tablespoons Galveston Diet-friendly sweetener (e.g., honey, maple syrup, or stevia)
- 1 teaspoon ground cinnamon
- 1/4 cup chopped nuts (e.g., walnuts or almonds), optional
- 2 tablespoons sugar-free caramel sauce

Instructions:

1. Preheat your oven to 375°F (190°C).
2. Slice the pears in half lengthwise and remove the cores and seeds with a spoon, creating a small hollow in the center.
3. Place the pear halves in a baking dish, cut side up.
4. In a small bowl, mix the melted butter, Galveston Diet-friendly sweetener, and ground cinnamon.
5. Brush the butter mixture over the tops of the pear halves, ensuring they are well-coated.
6. Optionally, sprinkle chopped nuts evenly over the pears.
7. Cover the baking dish with foil and bake for 20-25 minutes or until the pears are tender when pierced with a fork.
8. Remove the foil and continue baking for an additional 5-10 minutes to allow the tops to caramelize slightly.
9. Once the pears are soft and have caramelized to your liking, remove them from the oven.
10. Drizzle each pear half with sugar-free caramel sauce just before serving.
11. Serve warm as a delicious Galveston Diet dessert.

Nutritional Data (per serving):

Calories: 180 | Carbohydrates: 26g | Protein: 1g | Fats: 9g | Fiber: 5g | Sugar: 14g

Berry Bliss Frozen Yogurt Pops

Preparation Time: 10 minutes | Freezing Time: 4 hours | Portion Size: 6 pops

Ingredients:

- 2 cups mixed berries (strawberries, blueberries, raspberries), fresh or frozen
- 1 cup plain Greek yogurt (full-fat or low-fat, depending on dietary preference)
- 2 tablespoons Galveston Diet-friendly sweetener (e.g., honey, maple syrup, or stevia)
- 1 teaspoon pure vanilla extract

Instructions:

1. In a blender or food processor, combine the mixed berries, plain Greek yogurt, Galveston Diet-friendly sweetener, and pure vanilla extract.

2. Blend until the mixture is smooth and well combined. Taste and adjust the sweetness if needed by adding more sweetener.

3. Pour the berry-yogurt mixture into popsicle molds, filling each mold to the top.

4. Insert popsicle sticks into the center of each mold.

5. Place the popsicle molds in the freezer and allow them to freeze for at least 4 hours or until they are completely solid.

6. To remove the popsicles from the molds, briefly run them under warm water to loosen the edges.

7. Serve these Berry Bliss Frozen Yogurt Pops as a refreshing and guilt-free Galveston Diet-friendly treat.

Nutritional Data (per serving - 1 pop):

Calories: 60 | Carbohydrates: 11g | Protein: 4g | Fats: 0.5g | Fiber: 2g | Sugar: 7g

The Artful Tapestry of Dressings and Sauces

Esteemed reader, as we near the crescendo of our exploration within the inspired pages of "The Galveston Diet for Beginners," a delightful soiree of colors, textures, and flavors unveils itself. Welcome, with warmth and anticipation, to a chapter dedicated to the understated yet pivotal world of dressings and sauces. This is not a mere collection of recipes, but an artful tapestry where each thread, each ingredient, intricately weaves the culinary and nutritional ethos of the Galveston diet.

I stand beside you as a fellow connoisseur, ready to unveil the alchemy where simple ingredients transform into eloquent expressions of taste, adding layers of complexity and gratification to every meal.

A Symphony of Aromas

In this vibrant chapter, every drop of sauce and drizzle of dressing is a sonnet, a lyrical composition where the robust, the subtle, the zesty, and the sweet converge in a symphony of aromas. Each recipe is an artist's palette, offering a spectrum of colors and flavors to adorn and enhance the natural beauty of every dish.

Galveston's Whisper in Every Drop

With the gentle whisper of the Galveston diet guiding our creations, each dressing and sauce is a harmonious blend of science and art. Here, the nutritional integrity is as revered as the sensory experience, ensuring that every dollop not only elevates the taste but aligns with the holistic path of well-being we are journeying together.

The Dance of Elements

Prepare to immerse yourself in a world where the elemental dance of earth, water, fire, and air converge. Each recipe is a crafted balance, a dance of elements where the earth's bounty, the water's flow, the fire's zest, and the air's touch, unite in a melodious composition echoing the holistic harmony of the Galveston diet.

The Final Brushstroke

Are you ready, distinguished reader, to immerse in the elegant narrative where dressings and sauces are not mere accompaniments but the final brushstrokes, the nuanced details that elevate a masterpiece from the realm of the extraordinary to the sublime? In this chapter, each recipe is an ode to the refined, the elegant, the artful touch that defines the poetic embrace of the Galveston diet.

Creamy Avocado & Lime Drizzle

Preparation Time: 10 minutes | Cooking Time: 0 minutes | Portion Size: 2 servings

Ingredients:

- 1 ripe avocado, peeled and pitted
- Juice of 1 lime
- 2 tablespoons extra-virgin olive oil
- 2 cloves garlic, minced
- Salt and black pepper, to taste
- Crushed red pepper flakes (optional, for a touch of heat)

Instructions:

1. In a blender or food processor, combine the ripe avocado, lime juice, extra-virgin olive oil, minced garlic, salt, and black pepper.
2. Blend until the mixture is smooth and creamy. If desired, add a pinch of crushed red pepper flakes for a hint of heat.
3. Taste the creamy avocado drizzle and adjust the seasoning, adding more salt, pepper, or lime juice as needed.
4. Use this Creamy Avocado & Lime Drizzle as a flavorful and healthy dressing for salads, grilled vegetables, or as a dip for raw veggies.

Nutritional Data (per serving):

Calories: 160 | Carbohydrates: 6g | Protein: 2g | Fats: 15g | Fiber: 4g | Sugar: 1g

Tangy Lemon & Herb Vinaigrette

Preparation Time: 10 minutes | Cooking Time: 0 minutes | Portion Size: 4 servings

Ingredients:

- Juice of 2 lemons
- 1/4 cup extra-virgin olive oil
- 2 cloves garlic, minced
- 1 teaspoon Dijon mustard
- 1 teaspoon honey (optional, for a touch of sweetness)
- 1 tablespoon fresh parsley, finely chopped
- 1 tablespoon fresh basil, finely chopped
- Salt and black pepper, to taste

Instructions:

1. In a small bowl, combine the lemon juice, extra-virgin olive oil, minced garlic, Dijon mustard, and honey (if desired).
2. Add the fresh parsley and basil to the mixture and stir well to combine.
3. Season the vinaigrette with a pinch of salt and freshly ground black pepper. Taste and adjust the seasoning according to your preference.
4. Use this Tangy Lemon & Herb Vinaigrette to dress your salads, grilled chicken, seafood, or roasted vegetables.

Nutritional Data (per serving):

Calories: 100 | Carbohydrates: 2g | Protein: 0g | Fats: 11g | Fiber: 0g | Sugar: 1g

Spiced Honey Mustard Bliss

Preparation Time: 5 minutes | Cooking Time: 0 minutes | Portion Size: 4 servings

Ingredients:

- 1/4 cup Dijon mustard
- 2 tablespoons honey
- 1/2 teaspoon ground cumin
- 1/4 teaspoon paprika
- 1/4 teaspoon cayenne pepper (adjust to taste)
- Salt and black pepper, to taste

Instructions:

1. In a small bowl, combine the Dijon mustard and honey.
2. Add the ground cumin, paprika, and cayenne pepper to the mixture. Adjust the amount of cayenne pepper to your preferred level of spiciness.
3. Season the honey mustard with a pinch of salt and freshly ground black pepper. Stir until all the ingredients are well combined.

4. Taste the Spiced Honey Mustard Bliss and adjust the seasonings if necessary to achieve the desired balance of flavors.

5. Use this delightfully spiced honey mustard as a dipping sauce for chicken tenders, drizzle it over grilled vegetables, or as a salad dressing.

Nutritional Data (per serving):

Calories: 50 | Carbohydrates: 12g | Protein: 0g | Fats: 0g | Fiber: 0g | Sugar: 11g

Garlic & Chive Yogurt Dressing

Preparation Time: 10 minutes | Cooking Time: 0 minutes | Portion Size: 4 servings

Ingredients:

- 1 cup plain Greek yogurt
- 2 cloves garlic, minced
- 2 tablespoons fresh chives, finely chopped
- 1 tablespoon lemon juice
- 1 teaspoon honey
- Salt and black pepper, to taste

Instructions:

1. In a medium mixing bowl, combine the plain Greek yogurt and minced garlic.

2. Add the finely chopped fresh chives to the yogurt mixture.

3. Squeeze in the lemon juice and drizzle in the honey to balance the flavors.

4. Season the dressing with a pinch of salt and freshly ground black pepper.

5. Stir all the ingredients together until the garlic, chives, and seasonings are evenly distributed.

6. Taste the Garlic & Chive Yogurt Dressing and adjust the seasonings to your liking, adding more lemon juice, honey, salt, or pepper if necessary.

7. Refrigerate the dressing for about 30 minutes to allow the flavors to meld together before using.

8. Serve this creamy, garlicky dressing over salads, grilled vegetables, or as a dip for fresh veggies.

Nutritional Data (per serving):

Calories: 40 | Carbohydrates: 4g | Protein: 5g | Fats: 0g | Fiber: 0g | Sugar: 3g

Zesty Orange & Ginger Glaze

Preparation Time: 5 minutes | Cooking Time: 5 minutes | Portion Size: 4 servings

Ingredients:

- 1/2 cup fresh orange juice
- 2 tablespoons fresh ginger, grated
- 2 tablespoons low-sodium soy sauce
- 1 tablespoon honey
- 1 clove garlic, minced
- 1/2 teaspoon cornstarch (optional for thickening)

Instructions:

1. In a small saucepan, combine the fresh orange juice, grated fresh ginger, low-sodium soy sauce, honey, and minced garlic.

2. If you prefer a thicker glaze, dissolve the cornstarch in a tablespoon of cold water and add it to the mixture. Stir well to combine.

3. Place the saucepan over medium heat and bring the mixture to a gentle simmer.

4. Allow the glaze to simmer for about 3-5 minutes, or until it thickens slightly. Stir continuously to prevent lumps.

5. Remove the saucepan from the heat and let the Zesty Orange & Ginger Glaze cool for a few minutes.

6. Once cooled, use it as a marinade for grilled chicken, shrimp, or tofu. You can also drizzle it over steamed vegetables or use it as a dipping sauce.

Nutritional Data (per serving):

Calories: 32 | Carbohydrates: 8g | Protein: 1g | Fats: 0g | Fiber: 0g | Sugar: 6g

Rich Balsamic & Olive Oil Fusion

Preparation Time: 5 minutes | Cooking Time: 0 minutes | Portion Size: 4 servings

Ingredients:

- 1/4 cup balsamic vinegar
- 1/4 cup extra-virgin olive oil
- 2 cloves garlic, minced
- 1 teaspoon Dijon mustard
- 1/2 teaspoon honey
- Salt and pepper to taste

Instructions:

1. In a small bowl, combine the balsamic vinegar, extra-virgin olive oil, minced garlic, Dijon mustard, honey, salt, and pepper.
2. Whisk the ingredients together vigorously until they are well incorporated and the dressing is smooth.
3. Taste the dressing and adjust the salt, pepper, and honey to your preference. You can add more honey if you prefer a slightly sweeter flavor.
4. Transfer the Rich Balsamic & Olive Oil Fusion dressing to a jar or airtight container. Store it in the refrigerator until ready to use.
5. When serving, drizzle this delicious dressing over your favorite salads, grilled vegetables, or lean proteins.

Nutritional Data (per serving):

Calories: 153 | Carbohydrates: 3g | Protein: 0g | Fats: 17g | Fiber: 0g | Sugar: 2g

Thai-Inspired Peanut Sauce

Preparation Time: 10 minutes | Cooking Time: 0 minutes | Portion Size: 4 servings

Ingredients:

- 1/4 cup natural peanut butter (unsweetened)
- 2 tablespoons low-sodium soy sauce or tamari
- 1 tablespoon rice vinegar
- 1 tablespoon fresh lime juice
- 1 teaspoon grated fresh ginger
- 1 clove garlic, minced
- 1/2 teaspoon sriracha sauce (adjust to taste for spiciness)
- 1 tablespoon honey or maple syrup (optional)
- 2-3 tablespoons warm water (to adjust consistency)
- Chopped cilantro and crushed peanuts for garnish (optional)

Instructions:

1. In a bowl, combine the natural peanut butter, low-sodium soy sauce or tamari, rice vinegar, fresh lime juice, grated ginger, minced garlic, sriracha sauce, and honey or maple syrup if desired.
2. Whisk the ingredients together until they form a thick paste.
3. Add warm water, one tablespoon at a time, and continue whisking until the sauce reaches your desired consistency. Add more water if you prefer a thinner sauce.
4. Taste the Thai-Inspired Peanut Sauce and adjust the seasonings according to your preferences. You can add more sriracha for extra spiciness or honey/maple syrup for sweetness.
5. Transfer the sauce to a serving dish and garnish with chopped cilantro and crushed peanuts, if desired.
6. Use this flavorful sauce as a dip for fresh vegetables, a dressing for salads, or a drizzle over grilled chicken or tofu.

Nutritional Data (per serving):

Calories: 109 | Carbohydrates: 7g | Protein: 4g | Fats: 8g | Fiber: 1g | Sugar: 3g

Cooling Cilantro & Mint Pesto

Preparation Time: 10 minutes | Cooking Time: 0 minutes | Portion Size: 4 servings

Ingredients:

- 1 cup fresh cilantro leaves, packed
- 1/2 cup fresh mint leaves, packed
- 1/4 cup unsalted roasted cashews
- 1/4 cup extra-virgin olive oil
- 2 cloves garlic
- 1 tablespoon fresh lime juice
- 1/2 teaspoon honey or maple syrup (optional)
- Salt and pepper to taste

Instructions:

1. In a food processor, combine the fresh cilantro leaves, fresh mint leaves, unsalted roasted cashews, and garlic.
2. Pulse the ingredients until they are coarsely chopped.
3. With the food processor running, slowly drizzle in the extra-virgin olive oil until the mixture becomes a smooth paste.
4. Add fresh lime juice, honey, or maple syrup (if desired), and season with salt and pepper to taste. Blend until all ingredients are well combined.
5. Taste the Cooling Cilantro & Mint Pesto and adjust the seasonings to your liking. You can add more lime juice for extra zing or honey/maple syrup for sweetness.
6. Transfer the pesto to a serving bowl or an airtight container for storage.
7. Use this refreshing pesto as a condiment for grilled chicken, seafood, or vegetables. It also makes a delicious spread for sandwiches or a dip for raw veggies.

Nutritional Data (per serving):

Calories: 183 | Carbohydrates: 4g | Protein: 2g | Fats: 19g | Fiber: 1g | Sugar: 1g

Smoky Chipotle Ranch Kick

Preparation Time: 10 minutes | Cooking Time: 0 minutes | Portion Size: 8 servings

Ingredients:

- 1 cup plain Greek yogurt
- 2 tablespoons mayonnaise
- 1 chipotle pepper in adobo sauce, minced
- 1 clove garlic, minced
- 2 tablespoons fresh lime juice
- 1 teaspoon smoked paprika
- 1 teaspoon dried dill
- 1/2 teaspoon onion powder
- Salt and pepper to taste

Instructions:

1. In a mixing bowl, combine the plain Greek yogurt, mayonnaise, minced chipotle pepper, minced garlic, and fresh lime juice.
2. Add the smoked paprika, dried dill, onion powder, salt, and pepper to the mixture.
3. Stir all the ingredients together until well combined.
4. Taste the Smoky Chipotle Ranch Kick and adjust the seasonings to your liking. You can add more chipotle pepper for extra heat or more lime juice for tanginess.
5. Transfer the chipotle ranch kick to a serving bowl or an airtight container for storage.
6. This flavorful dressing can be used as a dip for fresh vegetables, a dressing for salads, or a condiment for grilled meats. Enjoy!

Nutritional Data (per serving):

Calories: 45 | Carbohydrates: 2g | Protein: 3g | Fats: 3g | Fiber: 0g | Sugar: 1g

Sesame & Soy Stir-Fry Sauce

Preparation Time: 5 minutes | Cooking Time: 5 minutes | Portion Size: About 1 cup (8 servings)

Ingredients:

- 1/2 cup low-sodium soy sauce
- 1/4 cup rice vinegar
- 2 tablespoons honey or maple syrup
- 2 tablespoons sesame oil
- 1 tablespoon fresh ginger, minced
- 2 cloves garlic, minced
- 1 tablespoon toasted sesame seeds
- 1/4 teaspoon red pepper flakes (adjust to taste)

Instructions:

1. In a small mixing bowl, combine the low-sodium soy sauce, rice vinegar, honey or maple syrup, and sesame oil.

2. Add the minced fresh ginger and garlic to the mixture.

3. Sprinkle in the toasted sesame seeds and red pepper flakes for an extra kick of flavor.

4. Whisk all the ingredients together until well combined. Make sure the honey or maple syrup is fully dissolved.

5. Taste the Sesame & Soy Stir-Fry Sauce and adjust the flavors to your preference. You can add more honey or maple syrup for sweetness or more red pepper flakes for heat.

6. Transfer the sauce to an airtight container or a jar with a lid for storage.

7. This sauce is perfect for stir-frying your favorite vegetables and proteins. It can also be used as a marinade or drizzled over steamed rice or noodles.

Nutritional Data (per 2-tablespoon serving):

Calories: 43 | Carbohydrates: 6g | Protein: 1g | Fats: 2g | Fiber: 0g | Sugar: 4g

Balanced Weekly Meal Plan and <u>No Waste</u> Shopping List

In this chapter, we present a straightforward, easy-to-follow weekly meal plan accompanied by a comprehensive shopping list to make your transition into the Galveston diet as seamless as possible.

Weekly Meal Plan
Given the Galveston diet's affinity for intermittent fasting, breakfast remains optional. You are encouraged to listen to your body. If you're not hungry in the morning, feel free to skip breakfast.

Daily Structure:
- **Breakfast (optional):** Depending on your preference, we've included a variety of light and nutritious options for those who prefer a morning meal.
- **Lunch and Dinner:** These meals are central to your daily nutrition, comprising balanced portions of proteins, vegetables, and healthy fats.

Hydration Tips:
Remember to drink plenty of water throughout the day. Aim for at least 8 glasses daily to stay adequately hydrated.

Exercise:
Incorporate a balanced mix of cardiovascular, strength, and flexibility exercises into your weekly routine to complement the nutritional aspect of the Galveston diet.

Weekly Shopping List
This list provides all the essential ingredients for your weekly meal plan, aligned with the serving sizes in the recipes. While it includes breakfast options, snacks can be personalized to fit individual needs and preferences. **Remember, avoid food waste!"**

Putting It All Together
The objective is to prepare balanced meals that align with the Galveston diet's principles. Keep portion sizes in check, focus on fresh and quality ingredients, and adjust according to your energy needs, especially if you're integrating regular exercise into your routine.

In conclusion, this chapter is a toolkit to kickstart your Galveston diet journey effectively. The meal plan is a roadmap, the shopping list is a companion, and the integration of hydration and exercise is the complete package for holistic well-being. Adapt, adjust, and align the plan to meet your personal needs and lifestyle.

Happy eating!!

Week One - Meal Plan

Day 1:
Breakfast: Morning Sunshine Smoothie Bowl
Lunch: Crisp Greens & Grilled Chicken Fusion
Dinner: Lemon Garlic Shrimp Skillet

Day 2:
Breakfast: Avocado & Egg Protein Boost Toast
Lunch: Zesty Lemon Shrimp Avocado Salad
Dinner: Quick Herb-Crusted Pork Chops

Day 3:
Breakfast: Blueberry Bliss Almond Oatmeal
Lunch: Sweet & Spicy Grilled Chicken Salad
Dinner: Spicy Chicken & Veggie Stir-Fry

Day 4:
Breakfast: Tropical Coconut Chia Pudding
Lunch: Herb-Kissed Quinoa & Veggie Mix
Dinner: Zesty Lime Grilled Salmon

Day 5:
Breakfast: Savory Spinach and Mushroom Frittata
Lunch: Mediterranean Chicken & Feta Greens
Dinner: Savory Beef & Vegetable Stir-Fry

Day 6:
Breakfast: Ginger Spice Overnight Oats
Lunch: Tropical Mango & Grilled Fish Bliss
Dinner: Garlic Butter Chicken Bites

Day 7:
Breakfast: Creamy Almond Butter & Berry Toast
Lunch: Refreshing Citrus & Avocado Greens
Dinner: Garlic Butter Steak Bites

Snacks:
Nutty Banana Breakfast Bars
Cherry Almond Breakfast Cookies
Minty Melon and Walnut Yogurt Bowl

Shopping List - Week One

Fruits
- Banana: 1
- Frozen mango chunks: ½ cup
- Frozen pineapple chunks: ½ cup
- Fresh berries: as needed for topping
- Fresh blueberries: ½ cup
- Avocado: 3
- Lemon: 4
- Mango: 1½
- Pineapple: ½ cup
- Cherry tomatoes: 5¾ cups
- Red bell pepper: 2¾ cups
- Yellow bell pepper: ½ cup
- Apple: 1
- Lime: 3
- Orange: 1
- Grapefruit: 1
- Mixed berries (strawberries, blueberries, raspberries): ¼ cup

Vegetables
- Mixed greens (spinach, kale, arugula, romaine, baby kale): 48 cups
- Cucumber: 3½
- Red onion: 1¾
- Kalamata olives: ¾ cup
- Zucchini: 2
- Carrot: 1
- Green onions: 2
- Fresh spinach: 1 cup
- Mushrooms: 1 cup
- Small onion: 1
- Onion: 1
- Bell peppers (red and green): 2
- Broccoli florets: 1 cup
- Snap peas: 1 cup
- Jalapeño pepper: 1

Meat & Seafood
- Chicken breasts: 4 (about 4 ounces each)
- Large shrimp: 1 pound + 10-12 pieces
- Boneless pork chops: 4
- Salmon fillets: 4 (approximately 6 ounces each)
- Lean beef (sirloin or flank steak): 1 pound
- White fish fillets (such as tilapia or snapper): 2 (about 6 oz each)
- Sirloin steak (bite-sized pieces): 1 pound

Dairy & Alternatives
- Unsweetened almond milk: 2½ cups
- Crumbled feta cheese: ½ cup (optional)
- Coconut milk: 1 cup
- Grated Parmesan cheese: 2 tablespoons

Grains & Seeds
- Chia seeds: 5 tablespoons
- Whole-grain bread: 3 slices
- Rolled oats: 2½ cups
- Whole wheat breadcrumbs: ½ cup
- Quinoa: 1 cup
- Almond butter: 7 tablespoons
- Sesame seeds: 1 tablespoon

Herbs & Spices
- Fresh parsley: 6 tablespoons
- Garlic: 18 cloves
- Paprika: 2½ teaspoons
- Fresh thyme leaves: 1 tablespoon
- Garlic powder: 1½ teaspoons
- Chili powder: 2 teaspoons
- Fresh basil: 1 tablespoon
- Fresh chives: 1 tablespoon
- Ground ginger: 1 teaspoon
- Cinnamon: ½ teaspoon
- Fresh cilantro leaves: as needed for garnish
- Dried oregano: 1 teaspoon
- Dried basil: 1 teaspoon
- Fresh rosemary: 1 teaspoon, minced

Oils & Condiments
- Olive oil: 26 tablespoons
- Extra-virgin olive oil: 10 tablespoons
- Red wine vinegar: 1 tablespoon
- Dijon mustard: 4 teaspoons
- Low-sodium chicken broth: ½ cup
- Balsamic vinegar: ½ cup
- Honey or maple syrup: 4 tablespoons
- Low-sodium soy sauce or tamari: 4 tablespoons
- Sriracha or another hot sauce: 1 tablespoon
- Fresh lemon juice: 4 tablespoons
- Fresh lime juice: 3 tablespoons
- Rice vinegar: 1 tablespoon
- Unsalted butter: 5 tablespoons

Others
- Egg: 1
- Coconut flakes: as needed for topping
- Grated ginger: 1 tablespoon
- Cooked cauliflower rice: as needed for serving
- Shredded coconut: 2 tablespoons

Optional Garnishes
- Red pepper flakes
- Sliced almonds
- Sesame seeds
- Cinnamon

Week Two - Meal Plan

Day 1:
Breakfast: Zesty Lemon Berry Parfait
Lunch: Asian-Inspired Beef & Broccoli Salad
Dinner: Sesame Ginger Chicken Stir-Fry

Day 2:
Breakfast: Fluffy Almond Pancakes with Berries
Lunch: Spiced Beef & Fresh Veggie Toss
Dinner: Honey Glazed Pork Medallions

Day 3:
Breakfast: Green Goddess Veggie Omelette
Lunch: Grilled Salmon & Asparagus Delight
Dinner: Cajun Chicken & Cauliflower Rice

Day 4:
Breakfast: Cinnamon Apple Almond Porridge
Lunch: Crunchy Kale & Roasted Veg Medley
Dinner: Lemongrass Chicken Soup Zing

Day 5:
Breakfast: Warm Pecan and Apple Bowl
Lunch: Tangy Lemon Herb Steak Salad
Dinner: Spiced Mackerel with Cucumber Salad

Day 6:
Breakfast: Sunrise Quinoa and Fruit Salad
Lunch: Cajun-Spiced Chicken & Avocado Mix
Dinner: Garlic Butter Scallops Deluxe

Day 7:
Breakfast: Refreshing Cucumber & Avocado Salad
Lunch: Classic Caesar with a Grilled Chicken Twist
Dinner: Rosemary Infused Lamb Chops

Snacks:
Cherry Almond Breakfast Cookies
Nutty Banana Breakfast Bars
Minty Melon and Walnut Yogurt Bowl

Shopping List - Week Two

Dairy & Alternatives
- Greek yogurt, unsweetened: 1 1/4 cups
- Almond milk, unsweetened: 2 1/4 cups
- Feta cheese, crumbled: 4 tablespoons (optional)
- Parmesan cheese, grated: 1/4 cup

Meat & Seafood
- Flank steak, thinly sliced: 8 oz (225g)
- Boneless, skinless chicken breasts, 5 pounds
- Pork tenderloin, 1 pound
- Salmon fillets: 2 (6-8 ounces each)
- Large scallops: 1 pound
- Mackerel fillets: 4 (approximately 6 ounces each)
- Lamb chops: 8

Fruits & Vegetables
- Mixed berries: 2 cups
- Broccoli florets: 2 1/4 cups
- Mixed salad greens
- Cucumber: 5
- Carrot, julienned: 1
- Red bell pepper: 2 1/4
- Green onions: 4
- Snap peas: 1 cup
- Mixed bell peppers, (assorted colors): 4 cups
- Zucchini: 2 1/4 cups
- Cherry tomatoes: 2 1/4 cups
- Red onion, thinly sliced: 3/4
- Asparagus spears, woody ends trimmed: 1 bunch
- Sweet potatoes, peeled and diced: 1 cup
- Kale leaves: 4 cups
- Apple, 2
- Strawberries: 1 cup
- Orange: 1
- Blueberries: 1/2 cup
- Pomegranate arils: 1/2 cup
- Avocados: 4
- Romaine lettuce, washed and chopped: 1 head

Grains & Seeds
- Granola, no added sugar: 2 tablespoons
- Chia seeds: 3 tablespoons
- Almond flour: 2 cups
- Cooked quinoa: 2 cup
- Pumpkin seeds (pepitas), toasted: 2 tablespoons
- Sesame seeds: 2 tablespoons
- Almond slices: 4 tablespoons

Oils & Fats
- Olive oil: 21 tablespoons
- Sesame oil: 3 tablespoons
- Coconut oil: 4 tablespoons
- Almond butter: 3 tablespoons
- Unsalted butter: 2 tablespoons

Herbs, Spices & Condiments
- Honey or maple syrup: 2 tablespoons (optional)
- Lemon zest: 4 teaspoons
- Lemon juice: 5 tablespoons
- Reduced-sodium soy sauce: 4 tablespoons
- Rice vinegar: 1 tablespoon
- Freshly grated ginger: 1 tablespoon
- Ground cumin: 2 teaspoons
- Chili powder: 1 teaspoon
- Paprika: 1 teaspoon
- Fresh cilantro:1/2 cup (optional for garnish)
- Juice of limes: 3
- Dijon mustard: 2 tablespoons
- Fresh thyme leaves: 2 teaspoon
- Spinach, chopped: 1/4 cup
- Fresh dill, chopped: 2 teaspoons
- Cajun seasoning: 3 teaspoons
- Cinnamon: 4 teaspoons
- Nutmeg: 1/2 teaspoon
- Dried oregano: 1 teaspoon
- Ground turmeric: 1/2 teaspoon
- Lemon wedges for serving
- Fresh rosemary: 2 sprigs

Others
- Garlic, minced: 18 cloves
- Salt and pepper: to taste
- Fresh coriander leaves
- Baking powder: 1/2 teaspoon
- Vanilla extract: 1 teaspoon
- Fresh parsley
- Fish sauce: 2 tablespoons
- Low-sodium chicken broth: 4 cups
- Coconut milk: 1 cup
- Red chili flakes (optional): unspecified amount
- Apple cider vinegar: 1 tablespoon

Week Three - Meal Plan

Day 1:
Breakfast: Sweet Potato and Spinach Breakfast Hash

Lunch: Lively Lime & Tuna Salad Bowl
Dinner: Quick Lemon-Herb Grilled Chicken

Day 2:
Breakfast: Minty Melon and Walnut Yogurt Bowl
Lunch: Sweet Beet & Goat Cheese Harmony
Dinner: Spicy Honey Garlic Pork Bites

Day 3:
Breakfast: Nutty Banana Breakfast Bars
Lunch: Spicy Southwest Shrimp Salad
Dinner: Tangy Balsamic Glazed Chicken

Day 4:
Breakfast: Ginger Spice Overnight Oats
Lunch: Roasted Veg & Quinoa Power Bowl
Dinner: Paprika Lemon Butter Clams

Day 5:
Breakfast: Kale & Kiwi Superfood Smoothie
Lunch: Sesame-Ginger Salmon Salad Delight
Dinner: Chili Lime Beef Fajita Bowl

Day 6:
Breakfast: Creamy Almond Butter & Berry Toast
Lunch: Refreshing Citrus & Avocado Greens
Dinner: Curry Shrimp & Coconut Rice

Day 7:
Breakfast: Cherry Almond Breakfast Cookies
Lunch: Mediterranean Chicken & Feta Greens
Dinner: Savory Rosemary Chicken Skewers

Snacks:
Zesty Lemon Berry Parfait
Fluffy Almond Pancakes with Mixed Berries
Warm Pecan and Apple Breakfast Bowl

Shopping List - Week Three

Vegetables and Fruits
- Sweet potato: 1 medium
- Spinach: 2 cups
- Onion: 1 small
- Mixed bell pepper: 3
- Red onion: 1/2 cup
- Mixed salad greens: 16 cups
- Beets: 2 medium-sized

- Cherry tomatoes: 1 1/2 cups
- Zucchini: 1 cup
- Avocado: 1
- Orange: 1
- Grapefruit: 1
- Banana: 1/2
- Kiwi: 1
- Apple: 1
- Cucumber: 1 cup
- Black beans: 1/2 cup
- Corn kernels: 1/2 cup

Proteins
- Tuna: 2 cans (5 ounces each)
- Chicken breasts: 10
- Eggs: 2 large (optional)
- Pork loin: 1 pound
- Shrimp: 13 large
- Salmon fillets: 2 (about 6 ounces each)
- Lean beef: 1 pound

Dairy
- Greek yogurt: 2 1/4 cups
- Goat cheese: 2 tablespoons
- Feta cheese: 1/4 cup (optional)

Nuts and Seeds
- Walnuts: 1/4 cup
- Pecans: 1/4 cup
- Mixed nuts: 1/4 cup
- Almond butter: 4 tablespoons
- Chia seeds: 3 tablespoons
- Pumpkin seeds: 1 tablespoon (optional)
- Sesame seeds: for garnish (optional)
- Sliced almonds: 2 tablespoons for garnish

Oils and Condiments
- Olive oil: 24 tablespoons
- Lime juice: 4 tablespoons
- Lemon juice: 3 tablespoons
- Honey: 3 3/4 tablespoons (optional)
- Maple syrup: 3 tablespoons (optional)
- Balsamic vinegar: 3 tablespoons
- Reduced-sodium soy sauce: 4 tablespoons
- Sriracha sauce: 1 teaspoon (adjust to taste)
- Dijon mustard: 2 teaspoons
- Rice vinegar: 1 tablespoon

Herbs and Spices
- Garlic: 19 cloves
- Salt: to taste
- Pepper: to taste
- Smoked paprika: 2 teaspoons
- Cilantro: 1/2 cup
- Rosemary: 1 tablespoon, fresh
- Thyme: 2 tablespoon, fresh
- Fresh mint leaves: 2 tablespoons
- Fresh basil leaves: 1/4 cup
- Ground ginger: 2 teaspoon
- Chili powder: 2 teaspoons
- Cumin: 1 teaspoon
- Paprika: 1/2 teaspoon
- Cayenne pepper: 1/4 teaspoon (adjust to taste)
- Cinnamon: 1/2 teaspoon
- Dried thyme: 1/2 teaspoon
- Curry powder: 2 tablespoons

Baking and Grains
- Rolled oats: 2 1/2 cups
- Almond flour: 1 1/2 cups
- Whole-grain or gluten-free bread: 1 slice
- Quinoa: 1/2 cup
- Long-grain white rice: 1 cup
- Baking powder: 1/2 teaspoon

Dairy and Eggs
- Unsalted butter: 2 tablespoons
- Eggs: 4 large

Seafood
- Fresh clams: 2 pounds

Others
- Mixed melon balls: 1 cup (cantaloupe, honeydew, watermelon)
- Coconut milk: 2 cans (14 ounces each)
- Mixed berries: 1/4 cup (strawberries, blueberries, raspberries)

Week Four - Meal Plan

Day 1:
Breakfast: Golden Turmeric Breakfast Muffin
Lunch: Herb-Kissed Quinoa & Veggie Mix
Dinner: Savory Beef & Vegetable Stir-Fry

Day 2:
Breakfast: Sunrise Quinoa and Fruit Salad
Lunch: Tangy Lemon Herb Steak Salad
Dinner: Cilantro-Lime Chicken Tacos

Day 3:
Breakfast: Green Goddess Veggie Omelette
Lunch: Spiced Beef & Fresh Veggie Toss
Dinner: Pesto Grilled Swordfish

Day 4:
Breakfast: Avocado & Egg Protein Boost Toast
Lunch: Cajun-Spiced Chicken & Avocado Mix
Dinner: Grilled Lamb with Mint Pesto

Day 5:
Breakfast: Blueberry Bliss Almond Oatmeal
Lunch: Classic Caesar with a Grilled Chicken Twist
Dinner: Pan-Seared Chicken & Asparagus

Day 6:
Breakfast: Refreshing Cucumber & Avocado Salad
Lunch: Asian-Inspired Beef & Broccoli Salad
Dinner: Lemon Herb Shrimp & Asparagus

Day 7:
Breakfast: Tropical Coconut Chia Pudding
Lunch: Crunchy Kale & Roasted Veg Medley
Dinner: Easy-Peasy Chicken Fajitas

Snacks:
Minty Melon and Walnut Yogurt Bowl
Nutty Banana Breakfast Bars

Shopping List - Week Four

Baking Ingredients
- Almond flour: 2 cups
- Baking powder: 1 teaspoon
- Eggs: 3 large
- Coconut oil: 1/4 cup
- Honey or maple syrup: 1/4 cup
- Vanilla extract: 1 teaspoon
- Rolled oats: 1/2 cup

Spices and Seasonings
- Turmeric powder: 2 teaspoons
- Cinnamon: 1 teaspoon
- Ground ginger: 1/2 teaspoon
- Black pepper: 1/4 teaspoon
- Salt and pepper: to taste
- Chili powder: 2 teaspoons
- Cumin: 2 teaspoons
- Paprika: 1/2 teaspoon
- Dried oregano: 1 teaspoon
- Dried thyme: 2 teaspoons
- Dried rosemary: 1 teaspoon
- Dried Italian seasoning: 1 teaspoon
- Cajun seasoning: 1 tablespoon

Vegetables
- Quinoa: 2 cups
- Cherry tomatoes: 3 cups
- Cucumber: 2
- Mixed bell pepper: 6 cup
- Broccoli florets: 1 1/4 cups
- Snap peas: 1 cup
- Onion: 2
- Avocado: 1 1/2
- Lettuce leaves: 8
- Red cabbage (optional for garnish): 1/2 cup
- Spinach: 1/4 cup
- Zucchini: 1 1/2 cups
- Asparagus: 1 bunch
- Carrot: 1
- Sweet potatoes: 1 cup

Fruits
- Strawberries: 1 cup
- Orange: 2
- Blueberries: 1 cup
- Pomegranate arils: 1/2 cup
- Lemon: 4
- Lime: 5
- Mango: 1/2 cup
- Pineapple: 1/2 cup

Proteins
- Lean beef (sirloin or flank steak): 2 pounds
- Chicken breast: 7 pounds
- Ground beef: 1 pound
- Swordfish steaks: 4 (6 ounces each)
- Lamb loin or leg of lamb: 1.5 pounds
- Shrimp: 1 pound

Dairy and Cheese
- Grated Parmesan cheese: 1/4 cup
- Caesar dressing: 1/2 cup

Oils and Condiments
- Extra-virgin olive oil: 25 tablespoons
- Low-sodium soy sauce: 4 tablespoons
- Rice vinegar: 3 tablespoons
- Dijon mustard: 2 teaspoons
- Cornstarch (optional, for thickening): 1 teaspoon
- Apple cider vinegar: 1 tablespoon
- Sesame oil: 1 tablespoon

Herbs
- Fresh parsley: 6 tablespoons
- Fresh dill: 1 tablespoon
- Garlic: 14 cloves
- Fresh ginger: 3 teaspoons
- Fresh cilantro: 7 tablespoons
- Fresh mint leaves: for garnish
- Fresh basil leaves: 3/4 cup
- Fresh thyme leaves: 1 tablespoon

Nuts and Seeds
- Almond slices: 2 tablespoons
- Pine nuts: 2 tablespoons
- Chia seeds: 3 tablespoons (optional)
- Sesame seeds (optional, for garnish): to taste
- Unsalted almonds: 1/4 cup

Liquids
- Low-sodium vegetable broth: 2 cups
- Unsweetened almond milk: 1 cup
- Coconut milk: 1 cup

Others
- Cauliflower rice: for serving
- Shredded coconut: 2 tablespoons

A Heartfelt Gratitude and Wish for Your Journey

Dear cherished reader,

As the final pages of "The Galveston Diet for Beginners" come to a gentle close, a surge of profound gratitude and affection swells within me, reaching out to you, who have embarked on this enlightening journey with trust and curiosity. Each word inscribed, each recipe shared, has been a heartfelt offering, but it is your engagement, your willingness to explore, that breathes life and meaning into these pages.

Your time, a precious gift, has woven the narrative of transformation and discovery, rendering this book not just a guide but a shared odyssey into the depths of wellness and vitality. Every chapter traversed, every recipe savored, is a testament to your commitment to embark upon a journey where nutrition, health, and flavor converge in a harmonious dance.

With the dawn of each new day and the breaking of every sunrise, may the principles and delights of the Galveston diet illuminate your path, casting a warm, radiant glow that nurtures not just the physical, but the soulful essence of well-being. Envision a life where every meal is a celebration, every bite is a step towards radiant health, and every moment is a dance of vitality and joy.

May the treasures unveiled in these pages be your companions, whispering the silent songs of wellness, guiding your steps with the tender touch of nutrition, and adorning your days with the vibrant hues of holistic health. In the dance of flavors and nutrients, may you find the melodies that resonate with your unique rhythm, orchestrating a symphony of wellness that echoes the harmonious tunes of a life well-lived.

With a heart brimming with gratitude and eyes gleaming with the reflection of your potential journey, I extend my sincerest appreciation for your trust, your time, and your presence in these sacred pages of discovery. May the Galveston diet not just be a nutritional pathway but a golden bridge to a world where health, vitality, and happiness flow abundantly.

To a life of radiant wellness, profound joy, and the graceful dance of the Galveston diet's embrace, I wish you a bon voyage. May every sunrise echo the dawn of wellness, and every sunset, the silent sonnet of a day lived in the full, vibrant embrace of health.

With deepest gratitude and warmest wishes,

Martha McGrew

Thank You for Reading!

I hope you enjoyed reading it as much as I enjoyed writing it. <u>Your support means the world to me!</u>

If you found value in these pages, I kindly ask you to consider **leaving an honest review on Amazon.** Your feedback not only helps me improve but also helps other readers discover this book.

Get access to your bonus!

Download "The Transformation Tracker"
and, for your convenience, the printable shopping list

Scan the QR code
or copy this link: https://o2o.to/i/ls2jK4

...and enjoy your bonus content.

Made in United States
Troutdale, OR
12/26/2023

16448661R00064